Hildegard of Bingen

Mystic, Healer, Companion of the Angels

Ingeborg Ulrich

Translated by
Linda M. Maloney

A Liturgical Press Book

THE LITURGICAL PRESS
Collegeville, Minnesota

Cover design by Greg Becker.

This work was originally published in German as *Hildegard von Bingen: Mystikerin, Heilerin, Gefährtin der Engel.* Copyright © 1990 by Kösel-Verlag GmbH & Co., Munich.

1   2   3   4   5   6   7   8   9

Library of Congress Cataloging-in-Publication Data

Ulrich, Ingeborg, 1929–1989.
    [Hildegard von Bingen.   English]
    Hildegard of Bingen : mystic, healer, companion of the angels / Ingeborg Ulrich ; translated by Linda M. Maloney.
        p.   cm.
    Translation of: Hildegard von Bingen.
    Includes bibliographical references.
    ISBN 0-8146-2132-5
    1. Hildegard, Saint, 1098–1179.   2. Christian saints—Germany- -Biography.   3. Mystics—Germany—Biography.   I. Title.
BX4700.H5U5713   1993
282'.092—dc20
[B]   93-19848
                                                                 CIP

Contents

Hildegard of Bingen

Born 1098, the tenth and last child.
Three stages: Bermersheim, St. Disibod, Rupertsberg.
Cloistered 1106
Took the veil ca. 1112-1115
Died 1179
Not canonized.

Visionary and Prophet
Student of Nature and Physician
Letter Writer and Poet
Preacher
Master
Nun
Sister
A frail woman
A vessel
A feather.

Works.

Translator's Preface

Ingeborg Ulrich's *Hildegard von Bingen: Mystikerin, Heilerin, Gefährtin der Engel* is a calm meditation on the life and works of the great German mystic Hildegard of Bingen (1098–1179). Hildegard is viewed at times from outside, in a third-person narrative, but more often from within, so that the story develops, to a great degree, from Hildegard's point of view. In preparing this English translation, I have attempted to reproduce, as nearly as possible, the tone of Ulrich's work and of the words of Hildegard which are freely quoted in it. I have also kept the annotation to a minimum, since an excess of explanation would disrupt the unfolding of Hildegard's life from "within." The notes are intended only as guides; the reader will certainly detect more references, both to the words of the daily Divine Office and to the works of Hildegard, than those I have been able to pinpoint.

The author has represented Hildegard's invented language in two different ways: for childhood experiments with language, she has used a kind of "dog Latin," consisting simply of a reversal of letters or syllables, while the invented vocabulary of the mature writings is reproduced verbatim. In translating, I have followed the author's practice.

The text quotes extensively from Hildegard's works. I have prepared this translation from the German text as given in Ingeborg Ulrich's book, with notes to the sources she herself used. In polishing the translation, I consulted the available English versions of the works to insure accuracy, but only in the case of Hildegard's poetry have I relied entirely on a published English translation: that of Barbara Newman, *Symphonia,* the use of which is gratefully acknowledged. Scriptural passages are taken from the *New Revised Standard Version* (© 1989, Division of Christian Education of the National Council of the Churches of Christ in the United States of America), with occasional alterations of person or tense to fit the context, or for purposes of consistency in inclusive language, which is maintained, wherever possible, throughout the translation.

7

Those who, after reading this book, wish more detailed information on Hildegard's life and writings are invited to consult the works listed in the bibliography, many of which contain biographical information as well as the texts of Hildegard's own works.

Linda M. Maloney

I

The Coif

The bands chafe under the chin, against the forehead. They scrape the skin raw. Blood beats against the roots of the teeth, against the walls of the vessels. Her head is bound and squeezed between her shoulders. To tear off the coif, lift her head, run in the wind, open her countenance, let her hair blow! Her hair—it has been cut short and rubbed with beech ashes.

The chin compressed to a square, the narrow lips, the forehead retreating beneath the coif, the curves of her eyebrows shimmer in the water. Now her forehead curves, the brows sweep up, the lips are fuller, the chin softer. Friendly water.

Being born and born again. Always the same tribulations, always the same desire. In my confinement, set me free.

Hildegard went to the herb garden. There was only a short time remaining before Vespers. The dill was as tall as a child and shone in the sun. She ran let her fingers glide through the feathery leaves, through the whirring umbels, rubbed out a few seed grains, sniffed them, licked the juice from her fingers, juice that can be dabbed on irritated skin, but she laughed at the pride of the dill stems. If it does not rain too hard, there will be a rich harvest. We will need it when autumn comes down from the north and presses its way into hut and cell. Clear lands for this, expand the fields, enlarge the beds. In my confinement, set me free. Hildegard bent down and pinched the earth. A dill umbel whirred across her lips. The bell tolled.

The Bell

Crown, shoulder and flank. The plectrum. The smith had heated the tongue three times. We cut up the time so that we will not get lazy; the cuts have to be clear and sharp. So says Criseldis, the bell-ringer. She has a piercing gaze, and hands that have grown thick calluses.

Criseldis had time in her innards. She had no need of the sky, with its sun, moon, and stars: constellations told her nothing, not even the bright star in the knee of Arctophylax, when it lay on the ridge of the roof. She did not need the hourglass with its running sand that hid death inside. She always knew when it was time to ring, and she rang clearly and sharply, so that the flanks trembled and the plectrum shrilled into the no-light, into the light, with a mind of its own. Oh please, line its sides with straw.

We allowed ourselves to be gathered, eight times during the sun's round, days of creation, day of rest, eternity; we let ourselves be disciplined, our body, our thoughts, our dreams. Criseldis let the plectrum shrill, the flanks tremble. Calluses covered her hands.

Hildegard envisioned time with the head of a lion and limbs entwined with serpents, and she waited for the hours between Compline and Matins, which she stretched out so that the lion's head crumbled and the serpents dropped away. Companion of the angels.

The Rose

Rest at midday. The stones of the hall floor gleam as if Teresa had fed them with honey. To try out how it would be to slide on them—but Hildegard does not. *O virga ac diadema purpurae Regis, quae es in clausura tua sicut lorica, sicut lorica.* [1]

It is cool outside. Hildegard stands on tiptoe, stretches out her arms; her fingertips taste the dampness. Only one degree below freezing, and this air will change to ice. Hildegard breathes deeply, takes in the air, sets herself on the floor and shoves her arms into the sleeves of her habit. How hard will the winter be, and how long? She goes step by step. *O virga ac diadema, aurora, salvatrix, Deus in prima die creaturae suae praeviderat.* [2] On the path between the propped-up bushes there is a rosebud that had not bloomed in time, but was preserved from decay. The veins in the yellowed leaves of the husk are rust-colored. Hildegard cannot smell anything; she takes the bud in both hands and it opens, petal by petal; its veins glow red. *Gloria Dei.* Hildegard is not afraid. Let the things that are closed bloom in my hands. That is a dangerous deed. I know.

If Volmar lay buried in this garden, I would break off the rose and lay it on his grave, but Volmar's grave is in St. Disibod. The blossom does not close again, the garden is bright, the day is already at hand. The bell rings for None, clear and sharp. Hildegard must hurry. *O virga, tu frondens floruisti in*

---

[1] O branch and diadem of the king's purple, you who are in your enclosure like a breastplate, like a breastplate. ("O virga ac diadema," sequence for the Virgin, 1a). Translations from the Latin originals of Hildegard's lyrics adapted from: Saint Hildegard of Bingen, *Symphonia. A Critical Edition of the Symphonia armonie celestium revelationum [Symphony of the Harmony of Celestial Revelations]*, with introduction, translations, and commentary by Barbara Newman (Ithaca and London: Cornell University Press, 1988).

[2] O branch and diadem, dawn, saving lady, God had foreseen your flowering on the first day of creation (Ibid., 6a, 6b, 3a).

alia vicissitudine.[3] The sun will not harm you by day, nor the moon by night.

[3] O branch, burgeoning, you blossomed after another fashion (Ibid., 1a, 1b).

The Decision

She hears her parents talking: she must leave home. Her brothers have been gone a long time already. She is a girl: why must she leave? She is still small, only eight years old. Her mother insists. Her father hesitates: he is afraid it is too soon, it might hurt her. They talk about tithing, about obligation. This child is intelligent: should we set her to cooking, herding sheep, turning the spindle, to wait until a man comes to marry her, a man who will have love affairs in the village besides? Jutta is a good woman, she will be kind to the child. There is room in her hermitage. Rarely has her mother talked so much. Why did her father not offer a powerful rebuttal?

Hildegard ran away into the garden, stumbled, ran back into the house covered with leaves, with a skinned knee, ran to her dolls: the king, the maid, the fairy. She talked it over with her dolls, but she said to herself: I am eight years old, how can you help me? I don't want to leave, I want to stay at home. How will I get along with this Jutta? Who is Jutta? She takes off the king's shirt, she binds the yellowed rushes tighter around the fairy's body, puts the king's shirt on the maid and sets the maid's coif on the king. Who is Jutta? The tall, dark woman who opens and closes her right hand when other people are talking, who opens and closes both hands when children bounce around and do not sit still on their benches. Hildegard beats the maid's head against her forehead; the king grins, the fairy collapses back into itself. Jutta is a nice name, though. Doesn't it have something to do with Judith? With the Judith who cut off king Holofernes' head to save a city. Jutta. Could she take her dolls with her? At least the king, or better still, the maid. Or is her memory playing tricks? Has she ever seen Jutta at all? There were so many people at the festival that time.

I still have time. It won't go so fast as all that. My father will have to go to St. Disibod to ask Jutta. Jutta will ask for time to think it over, and that could take a long while. Then a messenger will have to come from her and tell us definitely what Jutta has decided. And then—then they will have to make me a dress and a cloak with a hood to protect me from the rain. And then I will have to try to smuggle my dolls into the box, or at least one doll. And maybe it should be the fairy, after all. Hildegard took the shirt off the maid again and put it on the fairy, but it was much too big. A hair shirt. She had to laugh. A fairy in a hair shirt, what is the world coming to? And then they would have to carry a bed for her to St. Disibod—a bed, and what else?

Hildegard went into the kitchen, but Rena was not there. The fire had died down. There was a smell of syrup. She ran across the courtyard into the cowshed. The oxen had finished their day's work; they lay there, gazed at her, went on chewing. Gimbert was cleaning the plow and harness. Hildegard went to him and watched his motions. Why are you back so early, she asked, and sat down on the floor with her back against the ox's back, the one she called Romulus, took saliva from his mouth and rubbed it on her scraped knee; she would have liked to crawl between Romulus's legs. Now, how is it, what about you? Gimbert looked at her disapprovingly, but said nothing. Do you know Judith? No? Why not? The one who cut her man's head off, you don't know her? Hildegard was disappointed. She crept closer to the oxen, feeling the warmth of their backs. And Jutta, do you know her? The woman from Sponheim, you mean? No, I don't know her either, never saw her, only heard her name once or twice. Tell me what you know. I can't tell you anything, because

14

I don't know anything. She is supposed to be a good woman. Why do you ask? I was just asking. Hildegard turned around and laid her arms on the ox's body. I don't know Judith, or whatever her name is, and I don't know Jutta. But I know a little girl that had no father and mother and was completely alone in the world and thought: I will go down to the river, maybe a ship will take me across the sea to a lighthouse. Gimbert paused, picked up so much straw that it covered his face. Please don't let her go away. Hildegard laid her cheek against the ox's back and heard its blood singing. Oh yes, she is going away, a long way, the sun with her by day and the moon by night. One child begs for her doll, another for her curls, a third for her dress. She gives everything away. No, no, said Hildegard, she shouldn't give everything away, and the stars should stay in the sky. We can find another ending, growls Gimbert. She gets a new dress and sandals and a ring for her finger. And then! You can work it out yourself by tomorrow. Hildegard heard the oxen chewing. What is the ending, then? But Gimbert had already left. What ending? A ring for her finger, and then? Maybe Rena knows an ending. The beautiful stars can't be turned into coins. And I will stay here with the sun in the daytime and the moon in the night. She saw that Romulus was holding fast to her with all four legs, and she saw a tall, dark woman cutting off his head.

Coif, Bell and Rose
and Romulus the ox.
When I am confined, let me escape
into openness,
the sun does not harm
by day,
nor the moon
by night
the companion of the angels.
A fairy in a hair shirt,
what is the world coming to.
But the stars must not
be turned into coins.

II

The Mountain

A path leads up the mountain, steeply winding between bushes twined with honeysuckle vines. The breath comes short; stones pierce the soles, a magpie shoots upward.

The darkness inside the church is blinding.

Silently the monks enter, their habits swinging in rhythm. Bow and genuflection. Silently, they take their places. *In nomine Patris et Filii et Spiritus sancti.* [1] Bow and genuflection. *Quare tristis es, anima mea, et quare conturbas me?* [2] Kneeling down. *Kyrie, eleison? Kyrie!* [3] Rising up. *Vere dignum et justum est, aequum et salutare.* [4] Baring their heads, lovely faces. *Hic est enim corpus, hic est enim calix. Per omnia saecula saeculorum.* [5] The rhythmic swing of the habits.

They sat in the crypt with its worn stone floor, the verdigris-covered Christus. They laid furs over their knees, huddled their feet in them, drank hot beer with honey. Their limbs relaxed. Your candles give a bright light, they do not drip, their scent is like something from Arabia; we make our own from sheep fat, but I am going to try raising bees. The green of the statues fluoresces. Tell me.

> And I heard a voice speaking to me from heaven about five uncontrolled, wild, stormy, temporal systems of dominion: everything on earth is pressing toward its end. This is how it is with the world: existing and creating within the security of its powers, it is tending toward its destruction, pressed down by many dangers and heavy blows. [6]

---

[1] In the name of the Father and of the Son and of the Holy Spirit.
[2] Why are you sad, my soul, and why do you trouble me?
[3] Lord, have mercy? Lord!
[4] It is truly right and just, meet and good for [our] salvation.
[5] For this is [my] body, for this is the cup. Through all ages of ages.
[6] Quoted by the author from Eduard Gronau, *Hildegard von Bingen. Prophetische Lehrerin der Kirche an der Schwelle und am Ende der Neuzeit* (Stein am Rhein: Christiana, 1985) 130.

But the voice from heaven, a single voice. I will write it down and send it to you. Just now I cannot capture the blueness in words. Look at the shadows of your hands. One must always be skeptical. No ecstasies, no trances.

> And doubt seizes me, and I say, "it is useless." And again I want to fly above the clouds, that is, I want to get beyond my faculties and begin something that I cannot finish. But in the attempt I awaken an enormous sadness in myself, so that I accomplish nothing, either on the heights of sanctity or on the plain of good will; I feel in myself only the unrest of doubt, desperation, sorrow and oppression in all things. But I will not yield to the frail clay; I will wage a furious fight against it.[7]

I will write down the rest and send it to you. No more shadows; the hands held the empty pitchers. The light of the candles no longer reached the statue of Christ. Let us go to sleep, so that our marrow may grow again. When we sleep, our marrow burns because it grows and becomes fat and snow-white.[8] Let the closed thing bloom.

O virga, tu frondens floruisti in alia vicissitudine.[9]

---

[7] Hildegard of Bingen, *Scivias* I. 4. 5–6. See *Hildegard of Bingen. Scivias.* Translated by Mother Columba Hart and Jane Bishop; introduced by Barbara J. Newman; preface by Caroline Walker Bynum (New York and Mahwah, N.J.: Paulist [Classics of Western Spirituality], 1990) 114. (References to this translation will be noted as *HB*.)

[8] Quoted by the author from: Hildegard of Bingen, *Heilkunde. Das Buch von dem Grund und Wesen und der Heilung der Krankheiten,* translated and annotated by Heinrich Schipperges (Salzburg: Otto Müller, 1957) 152. Cited hereafter as *Heilkunde.*

[9] O branch, burgeoning, you blossomed after another fashion ("O virga," 1a, 1b). See Part I, n. 1 above.

The Fields

> When the marrow of the sleeper has increased and been refreshed, and the soul has renewed and reordered all the slumbering body, it retrieves into itself the mild breath that it had allowed to stream out from the marrow to relax the body, and so the person awakes.[10]

Hildegard visited a monastic farm. The fields snaked out broadly, in a multitude of precisely demarcated gold lines, uphill and downhill, gleaming with fruitfulness. We have made a plow, the brother explained, but it is still hard work. Praised be the sunset that gilds the fields and then lets them subside into blackness, as long as our sleep lasts to patch our broken backs. "Wheat is a fruit without blemish, but it does not make proper flesh and blood," Hildegard said. "You should plant more rye. Rye bread is slimming. Or try oats; they enliven the spirit and make the mind clear and bright."[11] She looked at the brother. He did not look as if he needed the night to mend his back; his belly bore the cincture snugly. We have the whitest bread, he said apologetically. We have refined the process of flour-making. And this oven here is built of special stones. Explain it to me more exactly, Hildegard ordered, but the brother shook his head and drew it between his shoulders. Then may I hear something about your beekeeping? I do not like our sheep-fat candles; they smoke and drip and stink. A clear, odorless light would represent progress for us. They had arrived at the cells. How happy

[10] *Heilkunde,* 155. For an English translation of some passages from Hildegard's medical books, and a commentary, see Wighard Strehlow and Gottfried Hertzka, *Hildegard of Bingen's Medicine,* translated by Karin Anderson Strehlow (Santa Fe: Bear & Co., 1988). The corresponding passage is on p. 89. References to this work will be abbreviated below as *Medicine.*

[11] Quoted by the author from Hildegard of Bingen, *Naturkunde. Das Buch von dem inneren Wesen der verschiedenen Naturen in der Schöpfung,* translated and annotated by Peter Riethe (Salzburg: Otto Müller, 1982) 17. Cited hereafter as *Naturkunde.*

they looked, these lay brothers. Hildegard tasted a liqueur made from honey. It is too sweet for me. She tried one made from herbs. Better, but it reddens the innards. And she looked back again at the golden light on the fields. The bell for Vespers rang; the fields took up the sound and expanded it. Criseldis rings more cleanly, thought Hildegard.

And then she saw, in the long, narrow chapel, the inward-turning faces with their lips consumed by silence. You have put gladness in my heart more than when grain and wine abound.[12] You make me to live without care.

There was oatmeal for supper. In her honor, they had put honey in the oatmeal, and with honey in the mouth, the water tasted like wine. Hildegard had to laugh. Asceticism, yes and no. Poverty. Riches. *Benedicite, montes et colles, benedicite, universa germinantia in terra.*[13] You make me to live without care.

After the night Mass, Hildegard fell asleep immediately. And in the morning she rode out early. A loaf of white bread, a bunch of candles, a pot of honey in her bag. *Benedicite, montes et colles.*[14] You make me to live without care.

[12] Psalm 4:7.

[13] Bless the Lord, mountains and hills; bless, all that grows in the ground (Daniel 3.53-54).

[14] Bless, mountains and hills.

The Cell

S he saw a monastery. The individual buildings were scattered about, old structures with crumbling cracks between the blocks, new buildings of red brick, reached by cobbled paths, walks made broad so that habits would not be soaked with water, would not drag through the mud and freeze stiff with ice. Big and small stones, spaces between; sometimes a foot might slip and be painful for a while. They glimmer reddish under the sun, and make the shadows blue as steel.

Stones gathered from the cleared woods, out of the plowed fields, carried here and set in the ground by hand.

The cell is narrow and all of stone; the high window blocks one's view of the outdoors. A bed of boards, a footstool, a table. When the dawn breaks, the walls press in on themselves. The candle drips and smells of rancid fat. The coldness of the stones creeps up the shins. The fields, the bell, the mountain, the rose. Everything together makes the whole. It is necessary to understand that, to think about it, to translate it into words. March, bad weather, wetness, ears, repentance. August, dew, heat, hands, tasting. Night and joy and ice and longing, snow and anger. The moon will not harm you, companion of the angels. Healing comes from knowledge, but the marrow burns.

> The world globe is kept in motion by fire, wind and air, and every kind of creature is sheltered within it. The heaven with all its glory encloses the upper part of this universe. But where would be the human being whose sight ever succeeded in penetrating such heights? The wide round of the earth, together with the waters that stream all around it, and everything that flows above the abysses, is all contained within the globe of the world. Nor can any human being ever grasp that. Finally, the abyss, with all its wonders, also lies on the base of this universal whole. And where would be the human being who ever succeeded in reaching that base? No one can do it, only God who laid the foundation. But the human being lives on this globe and is enclosed by its system. Therefore no human being's understanding can reach beyond this border.[15]

Ice and longing, snow and anger. It is cold, and the marrow burns. I cannot bring a warm stone from the kitchen, I might frighten the sisters. Lie down and draw the fur blanket over the face.

[15] Quoted by the author from Hildegard of Bingen, *Der Mensch in der Verantwortung. Das Buch der Lebensverdienste (Liber Vitae Meritorum,* translated and annotated by Heinrich Schipperges (Salzburg: Otto Müller, 1972) 44–45. Cited hereafter as *LVM.*

The Bear

Hildegard loved to walk across the fields on Sunday morning. To gather the body's forces and unlock the gate, open it until it allows a free view over the hilly field, fogged with the morning mist or golden in the sun. What a moment! She breathes deep and bites the air, grasps the field and lifts it up to her before she begins to inspect it: the orders are being carried out, the herbs have been left standing, they have not been destroyed by hail, rain, nothing has burned, they are growing toward maturity. She breaks an ear, pulls out the hairs, crumbles the grains, sniffs them with open nostrils, tastes. She swallows and smashes the notes of the lark back into the sky, lures the bird, courts with it high above, deep below.

Then the border of the wood breaks open; the bear is standing there, standing, looking, stepping cautiously forward. As this is happening, the song is choked off. Turn around, have the bear behind? Run away and goad it to chase? Stand still and wait? Go toward it, force it to turn back? What strength does she have, what power? She buries her fingernails in the heels of her hands. The bear ambles toward her. This is no crazy dream. Far from the walls of the monastery, no human being near, only the field with its low stand of barley that she had just been admiring. The bear comes closer, a big, muscular fellow. Hildegard stands still; her feet press down into the sand. The bear is getting bigger, it is a huge beast, lightning bolts dart from its eyes. It is standing before her. One must not look a bear in the eye. One blow of his paw would fell me to the ground. The bear sniffs at her skirt, creeps around her; at her left side he rises and places his paw on her shoulder, and Hildegard buries her hand in the fur behind his ears. What kind of tender touches are these?! She feels warm all over. The bear turns his face to her and she looks into his eyes; then he releases her and trots back into the forest without a backward glance. Hildegard follows him with her eyes until he disappears, warmth in her hand, wetness on her face. A weak woman. She has to think of Romulus, his warmth, his singing blood. To live in a cave, far from humans, from the weak and vulnerable. Security. Field, sun, lark, and a bear.

One day, when Hildegard received the gift of a bearskin from the abbot of Echternach, she took it without hesitation. And never before had any blanket kept her warmer than this fur. "Anyone who is too fearful must take a bearskin between the ears, tan it and lay it on the breast until it warms him or her. In this way, that person will lose all anxiety."[16] In the night after this encounter, she had dreamed of the bear, of its paw placed on her shoulder as if seeking support.

[16] *Naturkunde,* 126.

Rose and Mountain
Fields and Bell
Coif and Cell
and a brown bear.
The pelt gives warmth,
what kind of tenderness is this.
The marrow
becomes white as snow.
Land and cup are my allotted portion,
fair to me indeed is my inheritance.
Benedicite montes et colles.
You let me live without care.

III

Iris illyrica

Every day, during the midday hour, Hildegard went into the garden. It was quieter than usual then; she could hear the air. Sometimes she bent back her head and let the sun fall on her face; sometimes she bent back her head and let the rain fall in her face, on her eyelids, the tip of her nose, her tongue. She loved God very much; she opened both hands and caught the water, the sun, the air. It was well with her body, and well with her soul.

She looked at a dill plant, the bluish stem, the umbels with their yellow flowers; she nipped off a shoot and let it dissolve in her mouth. Not only against demons, she said softly; if we chop it up it could give more spice to the salads. She chewed a couple of seeds. And it would taste good in a sauce for fish, salmon for example. She will pass the word along. Not only against demons, not only for gout. I look at everything from the standpoint of utility. Look at the frills of the parsley that grows with the wind, smell the lavender, see the marigolds: they soak up the light for twelve hours, absorb it, and during the night they transform it, *sponsa solis*.[1] Hildegard stroked the radiating petals of a marigold with thumb and forefinger and sniffed it: this has great power, even against poison. Marigold wine. Usefulness and praise, praise and usefulness, I am a frail human being. She gazed tenderly at the fern that had grown so tall.

Clementia and Donata were already in the kitchen where ointments were prepared. It has to be stirred constantly, said Donata; otherwise it will curdle. Hildegard shoved her nose over the pot. It will make the heart lighter, I think. We need better fat, said Clementia. Pig fat would be best. Hildegard looked at her. Are we witches? No, we aren't witches, we have books, clear understanding, and a good nose. And the need to alleviate pain, Hildegard added, and she stroked Donata's

[1] Bride of the sun.

28

chin: you are grey in the face, and your skin is dry. And she took a ladle of barley porridge, strained it through a cloth and smeared the extract on Donata's cheeks, forehead, nose and chin; the remainder she rubbed on her own forehead. Clementia had left the kitchen. In the evening, the sister's face was young and healthy, and Hildegard's brow was shining. We really are witches, she thought, and turned to her prayers.

At the end of Compline there is a shriek. Reingard tears the veil from her head, rips off the bands, shakes her head back and forth, strikes it against the bench. Two sisters grasp her upper arms and drag the girl outside. Hildegard hears the blow. Like the dew of Hermon which falls on the mountains of Zion. For there the Lord ordained eternal blessing.[2]

Hildegard goes into the kitchen. The fire in the stove has already been covered. The wind is in the chimney. It takes some time before she can kindle the fire; she is not skilled in these things. She listens, waits for the water to simmer. Prayers lie between her lips. Then she goes to Reingard, sends the others away, releases the fetters on her shoulders and breast. Her face is grotesque. Hildegard knows what is wrong. She is silent. She supports the other woman's head. Drink. She administers lavender, myrrh, dill, puts the cup to her mouth, takes it away, is silent, holds her head, gives the cup again. Drink. Her breath is quieter, her features soften. Drink. The rule prescribes punishments, but Hildegard knows better. Be silent, put the cup aside, lay the head on the coverlet, stroke the left arm toward the heart, softly, slowly. Like the dew of Hermon which falls on the mountains of Zion. For there the Lord ordained eternal blessing. Reingard sleeps. Hildegard folds the veil on the stool and takes the bands with her to mend. There must be bands, there must be a veil against rebellion, against sorrow, against looks, against demons. Chastity. Humility. Warmth for our shorn heads. Reinhard's marrow burns white as snow. The mountains of Zion, the mountains of Zion.

[2] Psalm 133:3.

Hildegard went into the sewing room and mended the bands. The sun had set, but the sky still gave light. My stitches are still big and crooked; she thought for a moment about the altar cloth that time before, when the stitches were even crookeder under Jutta's gaze. If it had not been for Hiltrud. She brought the bands back to Reingard's cell, heard her breathing. Indeed, a portion in the land and in the cup. A goodly heritage.

In the night, she saw the blue iris.

The next morning after Prime, she went into the garden, looked at the high-standing bushes, held rigid by the sharp-edged, upturned leaves like swords. The remains of dried flowers that had been darker blue than the sky were still hanging on the stems. Hildegard dug up a bulb and cleaned it; iris illyrica; as drink or as powder it will clean the teeth and tame desire. She spoke with Clementia, who was tying up shrubs nearby. We should ask for advice, said Clementia, that saves time and work. Cook half of it and lay the other half on hot bricks to dry. Then we will see, said Hildegard, per-haps it has to be the spring bulbs, but that would be a shame because the flowers are lovely, and we ought not to miss them. Clementia shook her head; I really need a couple of helpers, a better stove and better utensils, but she said nothing, since the sister was always right.

Hildegard was already busy with her letters. Volmar sat with his back turned and wrote:

> Your spirit strains and shudders in great anguish when gross nature torments you with confused desires. You must escape from this seething! Hear, o human one: a man possessed a land that proved very fruitful. When the plow had dug the earth, it put forth with powerful shoots every fruit that was sown in it. It pleased the man to make of this land a garden of spices. Spice plants of the loveliest perfume should grow there, medicines for wounds and injuries. And the land was better than before. Now, then, o human one, choose between these the one that is more useful to you.[3]

[3] Quoted by the author from: Hildegard of Bingen, *Briefwechsel,* trans-

Hildegard sighed: reason, measure, strictness with oneself and others. She was glad when the bell tolled for Terce.

---

lated and annotated by Adelgundis Führkötter (Salzburg: Otto Müller, 1965) 62. Cited hereafter as *Briefwechsel*.

The mountains of Zion, on which
the dew of Hermon runs down,
there blessing will be ordained forever.
Sponsa solis, who transforms the light,
iris illyrica,
myrrh,
warmed on hot stones
bear it with you, with burned gold.
We are not witches,
gentle, soft and beautiful in color
the barley water softens the hard skin of the face.
The dew runs down over the mountains of Zion.

IV

The Haunt of the Jackals

A nd once again the silence of midday. A bit of sky, flying clouds, marvellous blue. Shadows of the cloister that
bloom and die. The others are sleeping, weary from prayer
and work and from taking food into stomachs made sore by
emptiness. Hildegard sat on the bench beneath the ivy bower
and laid her hands in the sun. *O vos angeli, qui custoditis populos,*
she hummed to herself, *et vos, cherubim et seraphim, perditum ange-*
lum qui volare voluit.[1] At two o'clock I will sing out loud so the
others can hear. It is good to be alive. The sun makes a sketch
of the columns, it is brooding in the ivy bower, continually
it encompasses foreign matter, the stone only remains intact
as long as the ivy keeps it from breaking, but a tree can over-
whelm even the well-grown vine, the tree it had protected and
nourished. That is how it is—friendship, enmity, *o vos angeli.*

But Hildegard did not get to the point of singing aloud.
Tiny, delighted shrieks attracted her attention. At the cellar
window below the ointment kitchen she stopped, bent down,
and between the iron bars saw a sea of cloth. The sandals had
fallen from the girlish feet; they rested on their heels, toes
spread. Hildegard tapped on the bars with her shoe and with
her ring of keys. Two startled faces turned toward her. Was
there any cubbyhole she did not know? She walked once
around the square cloister, striding over shadows and stepping on shadows, slowing her pace in the sunny spaces. Her
throat was as dry as potsherds. She saw her shadow tilting:
only then did she notice that she was still holding her shoe
in her hand. Her throat was as dry as potsherds. A broken
vow is a broken vow. "A woman who is so much on fire that
she cannot leave the world should not put herself in danger
by climbing a high mountain, lest she later sink into the

---

[1] O you angels who guard the peoples . . . and you, cherubim and seraphim, . . . the lost angel who wished to fly. *Symphonia* IV. 30 ("O vos
angeli"): 1-2, 14-15; 29:14-15.

depths."[2] The bell rang for None. Criseldis's fixed time. Hildegard went to the fountain, washed her hands, drank a mouthful of water, and hurried to the chapel.

Irmentraut had not appeared; it was good that she had not. Hildegard saw the rested faces of the other sisters; she tried to lighten the singing, but her voice wavered. She saw that her sandals were wrongly tied. Irmentraut was eighteen years old, a beautiful girl. Hildegard had noticed her high, taut breasts when they were hanging the wash. Should she send the girl away? What would her parents do with a child who was shamed? Hildegard thought of the disordered clothes, the feet in their delight. Who was the man? How did he get in? Is not every pleasure good? What did the others do with their hostages, with their wounds? What do I know about it? Iris illyrica! I am the one who takes care of them. Should I send her back to live a life in the world, to marry, bear children, raise them, and grandchildren too? Should I inform the sisters, talk it over with them, reach an agreement? What a nice meditation! Hildegard again sang one note too many, and Mechthild raised her head in shock.

Irmentraut was standing at the door of the scriptorium. Hildegard pushed her inside and closed the door. What a shining face! Is that the way evil looks? What shall we do, asked Hildegard, but received no reply. The natural drive, the desire for pleasure and the vow of chastity. *O vos angeli, qui custoditis populos!*[3] I am going to send you back to your parents, make yourself ready. I will inform Abilgard, and a brother can go with you. The girl was still standing there, beaming, wordless. Hildegard pushed her out. World to world, pleasure to pleasure.

> For heaven's sake, don't be dancing girls, don't just do as you please and be examples of the worst kind of morals! And don't be promenading around open doors because of your

[2] *Briefwechsel,* 213.
[3] O you angels who guard the peoples!

dirty minds, and beckoning lewdly in the fickleness of your dissipated hearts, as if you wanted to have in the street what comes in embraces. . . .[4]

At the end of Compline, Hildegard let it be known that Irmentraut of Stadland had left the convent. She had entrusted Volmar with the investigation of the cubbyhole. That night her sleep was shallow. Her throat was dry as potsherds. Her eyes began to burn. Lie on your back, close your eyes, the darkness is like a fur blanket. Irmentraut had been put into the convent without wishing it herself.

> When regret or sadness moves a person, the small vessels of the brain are disturbed, and the lungs as well. As a result, the small vessels of the breast and lungs send their juices upward to the vessels of the brain, which absorb them and cause the eyes to overflow.[5]

But Hildegard could not weep and soothe the burning. To be girded when the lion. . . . The lion was God. Drink the light from God's eyes. But the burning was not eased. Shouldn't I have sent her back? The child. The sisters. Cast down and broken in the haunt of the jackals.[6]

The burning of her eyes did not leave her even during early morning prayers.

> You must look at a green meadow until your eyes fill with water as they do when you are weeping. The greenness purifies the eyes, making them clean and clear again. One can also go to a river, or pour fresh water in a vessel and bend over it, absorbing the dampness into the eyes. Or one can take a linen cloth, dip it in clean, cold water and lay it over the eyes and eyelids, binding it firmly. The inner part of the eye should not touch it.[7]

[4] *Briefwechsel,* 213.

[5] *Heilkunde,* 231. There is a similar passage in Hildegard's *De Operatione Dei* I. 4. 32 (See *Book of Divine Works,* 107). For full citations of these works, see n. 1 to chapter 8, below.

[6] Psalm 44:19.

[7] *Heilkunde,* 252. See *Medicine,* 7.

But when did I ever have time to lay a water-soaked cloth on my eyes? Or should I look into a hollow container? And the green meadow? There was a storm coming; the grasses were restless. Hildegard was concerned about the hay. She went to Clementia in the ointment kitchen and acted as if she were smelling the fumes, holding her eyes over the steaming pots. A gentle mugwort or rose-petal or apple-blossom water. With thumb and middle finger, Hildegard rubbed her eyes from the outside inward. Her fingers felt good at the base of her nose. It felt good to close her eyes. But you have to keep your eyes open in this world. Vulture fat and deer suet are good for some things, said Clementia. When I mix powder with the flour to make rolls, they keep better. Yes, said Hildegard, but you have to bake them on hot stones or in the sun. Clementia nodded.

Cast down and broken
in the haunts
of the jackals.
Are we dancing girls, then?
O vos angeli!
O perditus angelus
qui volare voluit.
Look at a green meadow,
your eyes are dry
as potsherds.
Juices and waters,
salves and pastes.
Leap up
upon the scales
lighter than a breath.

V

Mirror of the Moon's Path

Disquiet. Horses neighing. Calls of "ho! ho!" Commands. Men come, carrying a chest that is so heavy that they cannot lift its feet off the ground; they leave streaks on the floor. Abilgard's veil flutters. Over here. The men tiptoe away. Here they come, the margravine and the girl. Hildegard extends her hands to them. The trials of the journey, muddy ground, robbers lying in wait, drafts blowing through every crack of the wagon, the horses are not as young as they once were and not much used to long distances, they were changed at the inn. The serving men stare around them, chatter, crack their whips. She brings greetings from neighbors and relatives. No, she will not stay in the cloister, but will spend the night at the inn, everything is taken care of. She has brought flour with her, and wine and honey and pepper. And the chest is full. Sheeps-wool blankets, bolts of linen, copper vessels, metal spoons, a roll of soft silk. Why soft silk? The margravine talks while the girl stands beside her, silent, her head low. The light plays in her hair. Yes, she would be glad to take a glass, a bowl of milk for the child. The woods are full of game birds, pheasant and quail, people seem to be raising more birds; there are pigeons, too. There are arrangements for farming trout, also; trout are more digestible roasted than boiled, and besides, they taste better. Fish, especially, twenty-four kinds, a great plenty. The margravine talks while the girl sits there with her hands in her skirt. There will be great hunting. Deer, roe, wild boar. There are plans for a tournament, but the rock fights have stopped; lances and staffs are finer, and chess! chess is part of it, too, and dancing, and we women will make sure the mood is festal. Yes, some pray and others fight, and then some others work. She would have liked to join in Vespers, but she has to leave. The trials of the journey, muddy earth, the laziness of the servants. The daughter takes her mother's hand, curtsies, still keeping her eyes lowered, silent. She does not weep at parting.

When quiet has descended, Hildegard takes the girl's head between her hands. I have to know what kind of eyes you have. And she looks into a greenness streaked with brown, sees her brows, the mirror of the moon's path, sees the brown-feathered green and is so enchanted that she covers the child's head with her two sleeves. That was the beginning.

Criseldis's fixed time. The bell rings for Vespers. Abilgard bound a cloth on Richardis's hair and took her into the chapel In the morning they will dress the girl, but she will not be changed. Bind the festal procession with branches, up to the horns of the altar.[1]

Hildegard could not see Richardis at supper, either. Ortrud read in a monotone. Perhaps Richardis would be good at reading aloud. Hildegard dipped her bread in wine. "Take nothing for your journey, no staff, nor bag, nor bread, nor money—not even an extra tunic. Whatever house you enter, stay there, and leave from there. Wherever they do not welcome you, as you are leaving that town shake the dust off your feet as a testimony against them."

There was still time before Compline. I really must have a word with her, thought Hildegard. I cannot leave her this way for the night. I want to know whether she enjoys riding, whether she likes trees, and which tree is her favorite; whether she has had anything to do with animals, and which ones; whether she had to help in the house and garden; whether she likes to dress up, or whether she prefers to run around like a boy. And whether she has collected stones or flowers or feathers or has knowledge of herbs. Why she wanted to be brought up in a convent. Or whether she was not even asked. Richardis answered in monosyllables, in such a way that no picture of her life emerged. But now she said clearly and unmistakably that she wanted to learn to read and write, and that she would rather sing the litany of all the saints than ride horseback, that she is comfortable at prayer, happier than she is when playing with the neighbors' children. She did not

[1] Psalm 118:27.

41

raise her eyes. And both were silent. Brows like moon paths, thought Hildegard, you are beautiful, my dear one, the flowers appear on the earth, the time for pruning the vines has come, the fig tree puts forth its figs, and the vines are in blossom. *Surge, amica mea, speciosa mea, et veni.*[2] Arise and come. After Compline, Hildegard said good night to them all more quickly than usual.

[2] Arise, my love, my fair one, and come (Song of Songs 2:10-13).

Silence

Walking on water. The birds are gathering around the house. Hildegard sees Jutta before her, tall and bright, Jutta who cut off her words when they were about to ignite an idea, so that out of her thoughts an idea would develop and become words, loud words into the ears of the others, not against the walls that dampened their sound. Jutta was silent, Jutta forced Hildegard into the prayer texts for the sake of ordering her thoughts, or the rhythms of the litanies, forced her words into Latin, where they became unwieldy in short sentences. Hildegard obeyed, learned to curb her delight in words. Our Father who art in heaven, so high and bright, give us this day our daily bread, in this straitened day, your will be done and is done. Talkativeness. Once Jutta fastened her mouth shut, her skin stretched, her lips thinned, the air burning in her throat. Don't cry. One who is silent creates no trouble. Silence is good for the soul. If you talk a lot you will not escape sin, death and life are in the tongue's power, said St. Benedict. But still, one must be able to speak, not only internally, without lips or breath. In my confinement, give me freedom. You are beautiful, my dear one, *speciosa mea*. Humility.

I, a pilgrim! Where am I? In the shadow of death. In what path am I journeying? The path of error. What consolation have I? The consolation of those who are pilgrims. I should have had a tabernacle adorned with five square gems, brighter than the sun and stars.[3]

Wherever they do not welcome you, as you are leaving that town shake the dust off your feet as a testimony against them.[4]

She would not have to fasten Richardis's mouth shut. She wants to learn to read and write, and to sing litanies. Time will make her lips thin soon enough. Richardis likes to be silent. I need not give her pain, pain that brings tears to the eyes when the band is taken from the mouth. A fairy in a hair shirt; what times are these; the naked king. Richardis had no dolls in her chest. O Romulus, always the last to be driven in, with deliberate tread, always the first to lie down, glowing with wellbeing; I lie warm between your four legs until Gimbert throws me into the hay. Silence is good for the soul. Silence is pilgrimage, said St. Benedict.

[3] *Scivias* I. 4. 1. See *HB* 109.
[4] Matthew 10:14; Luke 10:10-11.

Laughter

At almost the same time as Richardis of Stade, Adelheid of Sommer-Eschenburg, and Mechthild of Luchtenau came to the mountain of St. Disibod. The three were nearly the same age; they slept in one cell together, had the same daily schedule from early Mass to Compline, including spiritual direction, written work, practical duties in the kitchen, weaving room, and garden. Abilgard was a strict teacher, stricter than Jutta. When Hildegard questioned them once a week about what they had learned, Richardis answered in toneless sentences with pauses between the words, not uttering a single word more than she needed in order to pass. While doing so, she looked at Hildegard, and the green in her eyes was clear. Hildegard sat on the swing fastened between the oak trees, and swung as high as she could. The pines sang their answer; she carried the answer with her and swung back for a new question, in flight, rising to the heights and then braking until her feet found purchase in the earth and the pines were silent. The pine trees and Richardis's eyes. The green of the iris was changeable; it shaded into blue when she was merry, turned clear when she was thinking, and feathered with brown when she was confused: eyes that dismissed her or allowed her to plunge down into the soul, inexorable and full of relish. To let one's finger glide over those brows, and spread the lashes into rays. Brows, mirror of the moon's path.

In the evenings, after the night rest has begun, Hildegard makes one more round through the house. She loves the silence of the corridors, the closed doors, the end of the day. She dreads to hear groaning or weeping from one of the cells. But everything is still. Only in the room where the three girls sleep there is a suppressed gurgling and giggling; it lies deep in their throats and is swallowed, then bursts out in a canon, a chorus. Hildegard draws her sleeves over her mouth. She would like to go in and laugh with them, just so, only to breathe deeply. Only to live, as in those days, on the brook with the dove, until the sun sank its light into the water. But she keeps going, rubbing her diaphragm. The rule says that words provoking to laughter should not be spoken, and no one should love much or loud laughter. Rude jokes and any kind of idle talk that leads to laughter—these are forever excluded; we condemn them everywhere and do not permit the younger ones to open their mouths to such talk. The tenth stage of humility consists in not being easily and willingly prepared to laugh, because it is written that the gate breaks forth in resounding laughter. St. Benedict! Laughter is a healthy thing, it promotes respiration, and breath is life; it carries the blood through the tissues and muscles, the liver and spleen. It is true that raucousness makes the spleen fat. But laughter is from the heart.

They sit around the long table. Roricus is opposite Hildegard. He begins to wiggle his ears, just a little, only the tips. There is a tickling in her diaphragm. Roricus's earlobes are dancing; his ears jiggle and circle. Hildegard gets the hiccups. She does not know anything yet about the stages of humility.

> Before his fall, Adam had a voice like an angel's and knew every kind of music; he had a fine-sounding voice like a lute. But with his transgression, thanks to the serpent's cunning, there entered into his marrow and his shanks a certain wind that is still found in every human being. This wind makes the human's spleen fat, and unnecessary amusement, boisterousness, loud laughter and raw guffawing burst forth out of the person.[5]

Come, cries Mechthild, our souls are getting lighter and lighter; the mountain is dancing. But Richardis slips away; her smile dies behind her eyelids. Mirror of the moon's path. Saint Benedict! The sun will not harm us by day, nor the moon by night, amica mea.

When the girls entered the chapel for early Mass, Hildegard saw that Adelheid's and Mechthild's faces were clear, but Richardis had puckered eyebrows. Restore our fortunes like the watercourses in the south. Those who go out weeping, bearing the seed for sowing, shall come home with shouts of joy, carrying their sheaves. Like the watercourses in the south. Why were verses from Terce getting mixed in here? The cords of death, the torrents of perdition, the snares of death. God bowed the heavens, thick darkness was underfoot. God rode on a cherub and flew; came swiftly upon the wings of the wind. Hildegard was glad when the workday began.

---

[5] *Heilkunde*, 224.

The Boars

The boars strayed far into the forest; they drowned in one of the ponds; they were stolen. They are not very bright. Ratbert put chains on them: he fastened twenty boars on a chain and tied the chain to a tree. A hundred yards farther on, he did the same with twenty more boars, and another hundred yards farther he chained thirty boars. And Hildegard discovers it: she sees captivity, torture, confusion, forelegs tangled in other forelegs, snarled chains, snouts under tails, kicking legs, animals being dragged from side to side, backward and forward; she sees the sadness in their eyes, loss of appetite, pale ears. She weeps in rage and beats her fists against Ratbert's breast, hammering on it until Ratbert looses the chains and promises to think of a better solution: fences, ditches, herders. But he complains to the chief farmhand about Hildegard, and the chief farmhand tells her father; he has a talk with his daughter, and she does not attempt to climb on his knee, but remains standing at a suitable distance, and hears that she is not to meddle in others' responsibilities, she is to condone necessary measures.

Experience has shown that boars can accommodate themselves to chains, she does not know how docile such beasts are; they simply do not know their limits, appetite drives them too far and they do not know the way back to safety, they do not know where the pitfalls are, or who are their masters. But these animals can accommodate themselves to chains, and that is better for them than to be slaughtered by butchers or fall into pits. Those who cannot calculate the limits of their freedom fall into deadly danger. They need help. Hildegard stops crying; she hears every word and tests its validity. If a being is no longer master of its legs, its hearing and sight— what then? Then I will free it with my own hands. She does not see her father's smile; her gaze is lowered; she is cowardly. Come, says her father, we will go to Ratbert. Her father's hand is rough and warm: I will enter the kingdom of heaven.

The boars are lying peacefully, protected from poachers and traps. They will have to divide the chains more skilfully, says Hildegard; they can accommodate themselves to the chains, but not without any order at all. In my confinement give me spaciousness. The hand of the father, not to forget for all eternity. ''The globe of the world is kept in motion by fire, wind and air, and every creature is sheltered within it.''[6]

When Hildegard left home she would have liked to hold her father's hand once more, but the hand was on her shoulder, giving and seeking security. And she thought for a moment of the boars, who for a long time now had been running free again, since the chains had proved useless. She did not hammer anyone's breast with her fists.

[6] *Mensch in der Verantwortung,* 44.

Fastened in chains
the paths of the moon,
bind the festal procession with branches,
up to the horns of the altar,
they return with rejoicing,
carrying their sheaves,
not all laughter makes the spleen fat
be silent,
companion of the angels.

VI

The Circuit of the Sun

Day to day pours forth speech. *Gloria patri.* I will awake the dawn. An owl in the wilderness, a little owl of the waste places. *Kyrie, eleison.* They are like a breath. *Dominus vobiscum.* [1]

Hildegard had a capable group of sisters, and she did not meddle in others' responsibilities, she only remarked what was correct; she might say "take off more cream, so that the midday milk won't be too fat," "take more honey," "don't forget the parsley in the salad," "the bread is more healthful if the oven is not preheated," "bake some spelt into it," "lay the linen out in the midday sun," but she said no more than that, and the others nodded: Wineldis, Teresa, Ortrud, Donata, Alfriede. She sniffed the pots in the ointment kitchen, tasted, bound up a row of beans in the garden, was delighted with the tenderness of the stems. The leaves revealed themselves and were a miracle. Violet pearls. She called the gosling, fed a duck. But Volmar was waiting. The ground is exhausted, we have to plant clover; the wall needs repairing. It is time to make out a deed of gift, to inventory flour, linen and feathers, to write letters.

> Be careful that you are not sleepy by day. Instead, awaken your mind and do not utter two things, so that you do not speak differently within yourself than your outward sound. [2]

Your ways, your paths. They are like a breath. *Kyrie, eleison.* The sick are waiting at the wall, their heads full of vermin, with swollen livers and shriveled hands. Pain. Fear. Tears of hope. The most important thing is to give them courage. I am a frail human being. Alma is carrying on with the billygoats, working eighteen hours a day, taking blows from

[1] Psalm 19:2; "glory be to the Father;" Psalm 57:8; Psalm 102:6; "Lord, have mercy;" Psalm 144:4; "The Lord be with you."
[2] *Briefwechsel,* 120.

the servants, bean soup, beet greens, fleeing from the girls' room to the billygoats, not out of pleasure. That is why your skin does not heal, that is why your sores stink. Bathe. Drink. Don't cry. Hildegard does not hear the bell for Terce. Go home, stay in your room tonight, and come back tomorrow. Poor child. Poor man, eaten alive by vermin, clean your cottage and wash yourself in the brook. Drink. Take this salve with you. And then she shakes the woman who has aborted:

> Severe fasting and rough blows. Sorrow, earth, my cloak is torn, shudder, abyss, my shoes have grown black. Girdled with worms, you shall swallow fire and cast it forth again. Look in the mirror, see, look at your grotesque face.[3]

She throws the woman onto the bench. And hearing, listening, inquiring, reflecting. *Nec ego te condemnabo: Vade, et iam amplius noli peccare.*[4] She gets back just in time for Sext. *Et introibo ad altare Dei.*[5] Your ways, your paths. My desire lies open before you. *Et ne nos inducas in tentationem.*[6]

After dinner, a walk through the garden. Lift the face to the sun or the rain or the snow that melts on the skin. *O virga ac diadema.* Let the eyes rest on the green meadow or on the grey of the sky, the white of the paths. Smell a rose, a dahlia, a bare twig. Swing the legs like a soldier, like a tightrope walker. The feet stretch their toes. My desire lies open before you. Draw circles, ellipses, spirals in the water of the fountain, push up the sleeves, dip the arms in the water over the elbows. Severe fasting and rough blows, you shall swallow fire and cast it out again. *Nec ego te condemnabo?* Shudder, abyss, my shoes have grown black.

---

[3] *LVM* 82, 79.

[4] Neither do I condemn you. Go, and from now on do not sin again (John 8:11).

[5] And I will go to the altar of God (Psalm 43:4).

[6] And lead us not into temptation (Matthew 6:13).

Et introibo ad altare Dei. My desire lies open before you. To obtain the Lord's friendship. An owl in the wilderness, a little owl of the waste places. *Kyrie, eleison.*

After None, time for writing. Volmar sat bent over, writing carefully without looking up. Hildegard spoke in tentative phrases: and I—I who am like a quill—sometimes—and less than a quill—and am nothing. Volmar, with his level voice, repeated what he had written and waited. They worked two hours in this way, back and forth, without looking up, without thinking of anything else. But then Hildegard needed a breather; she waved to Volmar to indicate that he should stretch his legs, ease his shoulders, while Hildegard let her head and arms hang loose and tried to breathe from her solar plexus and rotated arms and head.

The singing at Vespers did her good; she thought of a melisma, a new cadence; her lungs expanded. Who turns the rock into a pool of water, and the flint into a spring of water.[7] To achieve the friendship of the Lord. Tomorrow, during the siesta, she will speak of liturgical matters with Adelheid and Mechthild. We must reserve more time for song sessions. God makes the wind blow, and the waters flow.[8]

They eat without haste. Chew well. The rye bread is delicious, not too fresh, the fish well seasoned, the salad refreshing. There could be a little more wine in the water. The pear is sweet as honey. Hildegard ate little of all of it, her stomach must first open itself to nourishment. She liked best to dip her bread in the wine, taking up the words and images of the reading, holding the cup with both hands, closing her eyes: there really was too much water in the wine; she smelled the food, heard the sounds of the others eating, felt the grainy bread between her fingers, wiped out the cup with the last morsels, crushed a pear seed.

At Compline there is stately singing, measured speech. In-

[7] Psalm 114:8.
[8] Psalm 147:18.

crease my worthiness. My desire lies open before you. Who turns the rock into a pool of water. Satisfaction with the passage of the day, confidence in the benefit of sleep, forgetfulness of a scornful thought, little desire for greater holiness beyond one's powers. Increase my worthiness. Day to day pours forth speech, and night to night declares knowledge.[9]

Then the walk through the silent house. Was the day not too long, the work too difficult, would someone in the night have to sob to herself, taking her cheeks in her own hands, embracing her own shoulders, stifling a cry in the blanket? Reingard had grown too thin, her shoulder blades were sticking through her dress; Clementia was already bent; Ortrud's lips were pale; Alfriede had back pains. And Richardis? Her eyes had a bluish cast. Brows, mirror of the moon's path. Close the cell door. Transfer one's remaining strength to the sisters, the farm woman, Alma, the woman who had aborted. The winged human, the right wing the good, the left the evil. The flight of thought, the height, the depth, the fall. The wings supported. And Hildegard falls asleep, half sitting, half lying, sees heads on the surface of the water, undulating, and she cries to the eagle to take her a short way with him, until she sinks into deeper sleep, letting herself be healed for the day to come. And again she wakes early.

What is it, then—the sun flees and we are cold, the winter is always difficult, we are so thin-skinned. Every sheep, every bird thickens its garment, but we, without a nest, remain in our thin-skinnedness. The cold runs under the skin, presses into our innards. I will collect furs and wool, we will sew shoes and knit a long scarf for every sister, something we can wear under our habits and take to bed with us. We will look for stones, big, flat stones, and during the day we will lay them in the fire in the stove and keep them with us during the night, we lepers with our thin skins, unable to produce warmth, shivering as we vainly beat our arms about ourselves. Stones, wool, pelts. The bear comes toward her, he is strong and

9 Psalm 19:2.

53

warm. Nothing can make me afraid any more. Don't go away. I cannot run to you. She has only the shadow still, and she must shake herself when the bell rings for Matins. Criseldis rings clearly and sharply, the flanks shudder, the plectrum shrills. Do not harden your hearts, as at Meribah, as on the day of Massah in the wilderness. Let the floods clap their hands; let the hills sing together for joy. Night to night declares knowledge, and day to day pours forth speech. I will awake the dawn.[10]

[10] Psalms 95:8; 98:8; 19:2; 57:8; 108:2.

Nec ego te condemnabo.
He rode on the cherubim
and flew
and came swiftly upon the wings of the wind,
the mountains rejoice in chorus.
The sun hardens the sapphire,
the river carries it,
she warms it in her hand,
she bears it in her mouth,
she steeps it in wine,
she tastes it.
Mountains rejoice,
on the cherubim he flew.
Nec ego te condemnabo.

VII

The Sapphire

Every jewel contains fire and moisture within itself. They originate in regions where there is a great deal of sunlight. When rivers in flood rise above their banks and their swells surge upward on the glowing hot mountains, these mountains, drenched with the sun, when they are touched by the floods, exude a kind of foam at some points where the water comes in contact with the fire; they glitter and flash, rather as glowing iron or a hot stone does when water is poured over it; and in the same way, the foam clings to those points like glue, and in three or four days it hardens into a jewel. And when the flood subsides, so that the water returns to its bed, the foam that continued to adhere to various points on the mountains dries in the hot sun in different ways according to the time of day and its temperature. Hence they receive their colors and powers according to the temperature of those times of day, and when they have hardened into jewels as they dry, they release themselves like scales from their many locations and fall into the sand. But then, when a new flood causes the rivers to rise again, the waters pick up many of the stones and carry them into other regions.[1]

A dry summer. It is unimaginable that a riverbed can go dry. Hildegard climbs down the bank: crumbling sand, withered branches, gravel, stones, big round ones, small sharp ones, flat ones, hollowed-out stones. She moves from one stone to another, zigzag, in leaps and hops, she is six years old, has no anxiety about her bones, has arms to balance herself, her feet tap the stones, the sun shines, Hildegard sings, sweeps over the earth and its hollows. No one can see her. One stone has red veins in it; she sits down on that one. Brought here from the mountains, carried, rolled, shaken, shaped, placed at her feet. She takes two stones and claps them against one another, holds them in her fingertips, rubs them around each other, bright, dark, sounding, echoless, but she can imitate

[1] Hildegard of Bingen, *Das Buch von den Steinen,* translated by Peter Riethe (Salzburg: Otto Müller, 1979) 28. Hereafter cited as *Steine.*

the notes and develop and add to them, there is a steam as when water is poured over hot stones. And then she sees the sapphire: it shines, and when it is held up to the sun its color breaks into green and orange. To see with the eyes what eyes cannot see. She holds it to her ear, smells it, tastes it. It is no help against sleepwalking. She puts it in her pocket, with the starflower and the feather, and adds another bit of gravel.

From this time on she was interested in stones, gathering pretty and ugly ones, washing, polishing, organizing them according to shapes or colors, building a wall of them, or a mountain, listening to them click against one another. But she carried her sapphire with her always, not only when she, without permission, strayed beyond the boundaries of the holding, when strange visitors came. When rage threatened to overcome her, she put it in her mouth and the anger disappeared.

One day, she went to Gimbert in the stable and asked him what he thought about stones. It depends, he said, everything depends. That was a riddling speech, and Hildegard did not press the matter further. Do you think they have a soul? Everything has a soul, believe it, and the stones have an ancient soul, both the bad and the good ones. Hildegard did not press this question either. She needed a hiding place for her things, and Gimbert showed her a hole under the floorboard. Then she showed Gimbert the sapphire. He was amazed, and he made a nest of hay and put the stone in it. You don't have to carry it around with you, he said, you don't need to do that.

> The sapphire is warm. It grows at midday, when the sun burns so hot that the air is a little hazy with heat, and then the light of the sun, because of the excess heat that it puts forth, only penetrates the air in such a way that that very light, under these conditions, is not so bright as it is when the air has cooled a little. And for that reason it is cloudy and also is more like fire than like air or water; and it represents complete love of wisdom. [2]

[2] *Steine,* 13.

The Crane

She is running across the fields, through the meadows; the wind applauds her, shoves her, tousles her hair, insinuates itself into her dress and lets it fly over a snail, past an alder branch, through a swarm of gnats, into a marsh that sucks at her, pulls off her shoe, clutches at her skirt, twists the fingers from her hand. She hears and sees nothing until the crane is standing before her with a stone on its lifted foot. No matter whether he is flying or resting, he always carries a stone gripped in his claws. Now he lets it fall, bows, flaps his wings, stalks goose-stepping through a figure eight, bows again, leaps several feet in the air and trumpets, dances to his own music, flutters the tips of his wings and strides away. Hildegard spreads her fingers and toes, imagining she is a feather; the crane returns again, moving in a feathery dance step and tossing tufts of grass, reeds and twigs around him; with his lower legs thrust far forward, he steps twice in a circle around her, trumpets and bows.

"The crane has a pure nature and is warm. It can both fly and walk. It likes to fly in flocks and so eludes pursuit."[3] It watches over the flocks, keeping awake at night by holding a stone in its uplifted foot. Should it fall asleep, the stone will fall on the other foot and so awaken it.

Hildegard picks up the stone. She is as light as a feather, can stand erect, has a base of grass tufts, reeds and twigs under her feet. The wind blows deeply into her innards. The crane has gone. She has only the stone in her hand, a stone with three edges and one sharp corner. She will keep it forever. By the time she has reached the edge of the swamp she is very tired; she sits on a tree stump, takes off the other shoe, drops the stone from one hand to the other. She would like to sleep, only for a moment, until her skirt has dried and is not so heavy. The sun shines in her eyes; it has already sunk very far.

The hour of Vespers is long past, they will have missed her, they may be looking for her; she will certainly get a reproof. Three edges and one sharp corner with a blue spot that shines

[3] *Naturkunde,* 106.

when the sun strikes it. She must go on, she dare not fall asleep, she will take the stone with her and put it with the others in the hole under the floorboard, she will not tell Gimbert where she got it. Is the crane trumpeting from far off? Is he whispering or snorting? A lynx creeps toward her on crooked legs, its eyes glowing, its breath laboring. Blood is running from its back. The stone in Hildegard's hand grows hot; she lays it aside, kneels, looks at the glowing eye, the powerful paws under the body, the blood, the pain, still hearing the crane's trumpeting. She pushes her hands beneath the animal but cannot lift it. There is a gaping wound in its fur. She takes the hem of her skirt to stem the blood, but the hem is crusted with mud, and her hands, too, are dirty; there is mud under every fingernail; her hair is short. The animal hisses and groans. How long has it been bleeding, who made this wound during the night? Doesn't Father say that spittle has healing power? But the lynx cannot help itself. Hildegard gathers saliva in her mouth and licks the wound, spits out the blood, licks again with her tongue and lips; she feels no revulsion, the blood tastes quite pure, she breathes calmly, gathers saliva, licks, the lynx lies still with a paw on her knee, its claws sheathed. The blood is stemmed and the wound shines in the tattered fur.

> The lynx is warm; it always follows its own will and does what it wants. It loves the sun and the beautiful, bright air of summer, but also the winter snow. It has very little resistance, because it is almost wholly dependent on the temperature of the air. And because it only does its own will, its eyes shine like stars in the night.[4]

The animal has leapt away. Hildegard wishes that her father would emerge from the bushes and take her in his arms. She picks up the three-edged stone and goes on.

> The birds that live in the air are an image of the human power by which human beings often propose and consider things in their minds before converting them into open deeds.

[4] *Naturkunde*, 133.

But the animals that live on the earth image the thoughts and deliberations of human beings that are actually carried into effect. The lion and similar animals stand for the human will immediately before action. The panther and animals like it represent the burning desire for something that is just beginning. The other beasts of the forest represent the plenitude of possibilities that every human being has for accomplishing useful and useless works. The tame beasts of the earth represent the gentleness that is in every human being when he or she is on the right path.[5]

At home, they put her in a tub and then into bed. Her nursemaid held the cup to her mouth, but Hildegard could not drink; they put a bit of bread in her mouth, but she could not eat. She called for the crane and for Romulus, cried for Gimbert to hide the stone in the hole. Finally, the nurse lay down beside her. It will be terrible if there is no one there to pick her up.

The next day Hildegard was sick with fever, her tongue was stiff and her body rigid. Her mother and the nurse took turns, her father stood by her bed and rubbed his forehead. She no longer heard the crane's trumpeting, no longer saw the glowing eyes of the lynx or the three-edged stone with the blue point. When, after six weeks, she awakened, everything was strange to her.

> The jacinth is warm. It arises from a particular type of urine of the lynx, for the lynx is not a sensual, libertinistic and impure animal; instead it has an even temperament. Its power is so great that it penetrates stones; hence it has sharp eyes and does not easily lose its sense of sight. This stone arises from its urine, but not in every case; only when the sun burns strongly and the air is light and mild and well-tempered. The animal rejoices in the warmth and purity of the sun and in the pleasant, gentle air. When it wishes to urinate, it digs a hole in the earth with its foot and urinates into the hole; thus the jacinth is formed and grows under the influence of the

[5] *Naturkunde,* 123.

sun. From the purity of the sun and the mild air that touch the animal and glow around it, and from its joyful mood and its great power, the urine is warmed within it. When, under these conditions, it is released, it crystallizes into this stone, in such a way that the hardening of this lovely gem, which is softer than other stones, takes place within the earth.[6]

Hildegard's father sometimes took her on his knee, lifted her up like a feather, set her down and loosened his jacket. When you grow up we will go hunting together, shoot partridges and rabbits, foxes and wildcats. But Hildegard thought about the crane's bowing motions and the claws of the lynx that had rested on her knee. Finally she could go to the stable again to place her stone with the blue point beside the sapphire and stamp the floorboard firmly into place. When Romulus snorted she had to laugh, and when Gimbert heard it he took her on his shoulders and danced with her between the cows. And Romulus snorted again.

[6] *Steine,* 68.

Water

Hildegard was well again, and renewed her intimacy with strange things. Sometimes she went to the brook behind the house that brought fresh water, thrust her legs into it, moving her feet and feeling herself strengthened so that even the roots of her hair felt alive. Or she watched the water, how it flowed and divided, gurgling around the stone and then closing together again. She set a nutshell on the water and watched it being carried away. Her brothers could skip stones across the water, and Hildegard watched the circles appear and expand, dissolving into infinity.

One day she hurt her hand while playing. She did not want to lick off the blood, but held her hand in the water and saw how the stream took the blood with it, felt the pain flowing away also. The wound closed, and only a redness remained.

> Water has fifteen powers: warmth, airiness, moistness, surging, speed, mobility; in addition, it gives sap to the trees, taste to the fruit, and gives the herbs their green power; its moisture soaks into all things: it sustains the birds, feeds the fish, with its warmth it gives life to the animals, it retains the creeping things within its slime, and so it holds all things together. For from the sources of life spring the waters that wash away all dishonesty. It is water that, in every creature capable of movement, is so easily moved, and that, even in the immovable parts of creation, is the driving force for all the power of greenness. Water holds and maintains everything by its powers.[7]

She sees a waterfall that sinks and replenishes itself; sees how the lame are washed in the water and can walk again, how lepers are dipped in the water and are clean. And the waterfall sinks and replenishes itself and shines.

Now she had confident knowledge; she treated her wounds, whether burns from the kitchen or from the autumn fires, cuts or bruises, with water from the brook or the well, and she was enraptured when the pain subsided.

Water of east and west, of south and north, water of wells and brooks, fountains and rivers and of the great ocean that surrounds the earth.

On the sea and the great rivers one can sail. Before Hildegard left her parents' house for good, she was allowed to make a request, and she asked for a ride in a boat. Her mother feared she would be ill again, but her father said that a wish was a wish, and they had promised to fulfill it, and he had the last word. But he could not go with her, and so she went alone with the ferryman. On the outward journey, her feet placed alongside one another, her hands in her lap, she feels that her body is weightless, as the house, the meadows with their

[7] *Heilkunde*, 77.

trees, the pastures slip away. Something that is yielding and without bottom, yet supports. Hildegard lies on her back, feeling the support, seeing the sky and the evening star that accompanies her. She begins to sing. The ferryman joins her, and so does the sky with its evening star and all the waters, those of the east and west, the south and north, of the wells and brooks, fountains and rivers and the great ocean that surrounds the world. The floods have lifted up their voice, the floods lift up their roaring. More majestic than the thunder of mighty waters, more majestic than the waves of the sea, majestic on high is the Lord.[8]

[8] Psalm 93:3-4.

The waters of
east and south
in streams and brooks
bring the stones
hardened by the sun,
the crane holds the sapphire
on a raised foot,
the commandments are trustworthy.

VIII

Hands

The lynx's paw on her knee, the bigger paw of the bear on her shoulder. With his huge hands, Gimbert spreads hay for the cows, grips the wings of the swing, always ready to catch the child. The sure hands of the nursemaid, the cool hands of her mother in the feverish night, and the hand of her father that engulfs Hildegard's hand and rests on it, giving and seeking security. Jutta opens and closes her hands, hands made up of bones and spidery veins.

> The eighth month approaches in full force like a mighty ruler who governs his whole realm in the plenitude of his power. Hence, joy shines forth from it. Burning in its course with the scorching sun, it possesses a certain moisture and therefore brings dew as well. It can also bring terrible thunderstorms, because the sun is again tending toward its decline. The characteristics of this month are reflected in human hands. It is the hands that work; they unite and store within themselves the power of the whole body. From the work of these hands, the human being often gains fame. Gifted with knowledge, the human being can exclude what is dangerous and useless, while retaining what is good and useful, just as the hands complete their laudable arrangements with strength and propriety, like artists who, out of their creative talent, arrange every part of their houses in such a way that in them they wisely bring to expression their whole being.[1]

Bowls that catch sun and rain, and toss a field into the skies, cause a rose found in winter to bloom: hands that within them-

---

[1] Cited by the author from: Hildegard of Bingen, *Welt und Mensch. Das Buch "De Operatione Dei,"* translated and annotated by Heinrich Schipperges (Salzburg: Otto Müller, 1965) 158–59. Hereafter cited as *De Operatione Dei.* For an English translation of portions of this book (not including this section on the months of the year), see: *Hildegard of Bingen's Book of Divine Works with Letters and Songs,* edited and introduced by Matthew Fox (Santa Fe: Bear & Co., 1987), which will be cited as *Book of Divine Works.*

selves join and store the power of the whole body. Hildegard likes to keep them hidden in the sleeves of her habit, gripping her elbows, not only when going to chapel, during the readings, and when singing the litanies, but also when she is dictating, when she herself is not sketching something along with the others, and when listening to a complaint; even in the garden, when there is nothing to be put in order there.

Prayer and work and rest and prayer and work, that is a good rhythm, Hildegard says to Clementia, who is plucking watercress. You should take some of it to the kitchen for our salad, it would be good for our gums. You could also rub some of the juice from the cress on your hands, you are getting some brown spots.

I should be helping her, she thinks, but she cannot draw her hands out of the sleeves. August, a powerful ruler who enflames the dahlias and fires the sunflowers; it possesses its realm. When a thunderstorm comes it will cut off their heads, we must be careful about the seeds. But Clementia does not even say that rain would be useful; she takes her basket, puts her hand on Hildegard's shoulder and goes away. Silence, prayer, work and silence.

Companion of the angels.

> In exchange for riches, a man promised the devil what was standing behind his house, namely his apple tree; but behind his house stood his daughter. However, the devil could not approach the maiden, not even when her father cut off her hands. Later, the king whom she had found had silver hands made for her. But then the king had to go to war, and the queen was banished, because the devil was still at work. For seven years the king sought his wife and found her in a tiny cottage on which was a little sign with the words, "everyone may live in freedom here." In those seven years, the queen had received her living hands back again. "My wife has silver hands," said the king. She answered: "The gracious God has let my natural hands grow back again," and an angel went into her chamber, brought the silver hands and showed them to the king. Then he saw for certain that she was his

dear wife, and he kissed her and was happy. And they lived happily until their blessed end.

Hildegard sighed, set five fingertips on five fingertips and dipped them in the water of the fountain; her heart shuddered for a moment. Water from east and west, from south and north, from wells and brooks, fountains and rivers, water of the ocean that surrounds the whole world, the meadows and pastures glide away. The plectrum shrills, the flanks shudder, Criseldis rings sharp and clear. The floods have lifted up their voice. More majestic than the thunder of mighty waters, more majestic than the waves of the sea. Your decrees are very sure. He comes in the fullness of power, like a mighty ruler, girded, who governs his realm in the plenitude of his might, so the earth is set on its foundations and shall not be shaken. And joy streams from him. [2]

After None, Hildegard did not come as agreed into the writing room. A mother was there with her child, asking for help. The child has been dumb for thirty days. Why should someone not keep silent for three or three hundred days, thinks Hildegard, and looks at the child, sees the strained and distorted mouth vainly trying to speak. Hildegard tells the child the story of the girl without hands, tells it of the silver hands and the hands that grew back again. The child wants to ask something, but it can utter not a syllable, not a sound. Hildegard brings a cup of water, holds the cup in her hands, and says: Drink! It will do you good, you are thirsty after the long journey. Drink! And the child lays its hand on Hildegard's hand, the one holding the cup; it had never before tasted such good water. Why should the child not be able to speak again? After all, it is alive. It wants another swallow, and still another. And the lips form a little smile, the cheeks redden, the eyes reflect Hildegard's tenderness, and then come the words: about the bread it would like to eat, of the father with whom it will go into the forest again tomorrow to pick berries. And it will fly

[2] Cf. Psalms 93:3-5; 104:5.

with the butterflies. And Hildegard says yes, yes, fly with the butterflies. Now go home and be happy.

She is a little dizzy. She puts the cup aside, slips her hands into the sleeves of her habit, up to the shoulders, and walks slowly to the scriptorium. Dear Volmar.

Volmar

There he sits, her scribe, advisor, teacher, provost, her friend. His hood has fallen back; his tonsured hair is growing gray. He has big ears. She knows that. When his hood drops back, she sees his left ear in the grilled window. Probably his feet are set straight; perhaps his cincture is shining. She cannot even see his hands. He does not look up. Does he not sense the dizziness in her? What she would really like to do is run into the garden in her bare feet, feel the gravel, pull the weeds, clean the well water.

> The walnut tree is warm and bitter. Before it bears its fruit, the warmth and bitterness are seated in the trunk and leaves. The bitterness emits the warmth and brings forth the nuts. As soon as the nuts begin to grow, the bitterness recedes, and a sweetness arises. When the sweetness has entered into the fruits, the bitterness and warmth remain behind, in the trunk. As soon as the fruits have grown and ripened, the leaves, as on all fruit-bearing trees, possess no more healing power, since their juice has been transferred to the fruit. For that reason one should break the leaves from the tree before any fruit grows on it.[3]

Now it was Volmar's turn. He repeated what he had written, hunted for an appropriate word, revised the sentence, repeated it. No, said Hildegard, the sentence, "as soon as the nuts begin to grow, the bitterness recedes, and a sweet-

[3] *Naturkunde,* 65.

ness arises," must remain as it is. And Volmar corrects again. When he has read everything in full context, Hildegard continues with the applications against worms, leprosy, gout, scabs on the scalp—provided, first of all, that God is not opposed. This, she says, you can formulate however you wish, and she leaned back and looked at Volmar's ear. Would he have preferred to remain at St. Disibod, to do his own work and be the head of a monastery? She sees him supervising construction, measuring a field, directing the harvesting of the grapes and the working of the winepress, laying out a herb garden and directing the trimming, sampling the products of the bakery. And she smiled. No, dear Volmar, you cannot do all that; I can do it better, but you can listen with your big ears, you can construct sentences and write very neatly. She looked at the gray ring of hair on his head, and warm blood surged into her heart.

Volmar looked up. We can still do the chestnut tree, said Hildegard. "It is very warm, and because of its warmth possesses great power. It represents discretion. Its juices and its fruit are useful against every kind of human weakness."[4]— She allowed Volmar some time. We should drink a cup of chestnut sap together, she thought, but then she continued:

> Anyone who suffers from gout and is angry—for gout is always accompanied by anger—and repeatedly prepares steam baths of the chestnut's leaves, bark and fruits, will lose the gout and recover a gentle temperament. Against animal plagues, one should frequently give the crushed bark of the chestnut to the asses, horses, oxen, sheep, swine, and all other cattle in their drink.[5]

She had learned this last item from Ratbert; she can see him now, grating the bark and calling out to her to stand aside so that a sliver will not fly into her eye; she starts as Volmar clears his throat and says softly:

[4] *Naturkunde,* 68-69. See *Medicine,* 71.
[5] *Naturkunde,* 68-69. See *Medicine,* 110, where the translation refers to arthritis rather than gout.

> If one cuts a staff from chestnut wood and holds it in the hand
> in such a way that the hand is warmed by it, in absorbing
> the warmth one gains a strengthening of the veins and of all
> the powers. Smelling the wood brings health to the head.[6]

What does "all the powers" mean, asked Volmar. Just that: "all the powers." That part about the staff must certainly be included. Is Volmar shaking his head? That about smelling, too. That is important.

When the writing session was over, she said: we cannot plant any more chestnut trees, but there may be some that we can buy. Then we will cut staffs for the pilgrims who stop here, and for ourselves. But Volmar did not react; he was busy making corrections.

That night, Hildegard cannot sleep. She seems to drift off quickly, but in an hour's time her exhaustion has been overcome. The night is dark, without moon or stars. Even the wind seems to have died. She pulls the bearskin higher. The walls of her cell are closing in on her. Gout and anger, August and hands, bitterness and sweetness, once the fruits have ripened the leaves lose their healing power. She lies on her back, her hands laid across her body, she feels warmth, sniffs at the fur, the bear comes out of the forest and walks toward her. The child will go into the forest with its father today, and catch butterflies.

> All the trees, like the grasses, contain warmth and coldness
> within themselves; some are warmer, others colder. All trees
> bear fruit; those with proper fruits are more cold than warm.
> The trees of the forest are among these.[7]

The chestnut tree and reticence. But the human being lives on this earthly globe and is enclosed by its circling. Where would that human being be, who ever could reach the bottom of things?

[6] *Naturkunde,* 68–69.
[7] *Naturkunde,* 64.

There is a soft, hesitant tapping, like fingertips. Is someone in distress? Is the farmer's wife at Eschhof about to bear her child and in need of help? Is it Richardis? It is in my head, I must sleep. The tapping comes again. Who is there in this house who cannot sleep and is creeping about in the night? Hildegard feels her breath dividing the hairs of the bearskin. Timidity is not a virtue. She stands up and goes to the window. Is that Volmar's face in the darkness? What has happened? The window cannot be opened, she cannot understand what is being whispered, sets her ear against the glass, the glass is smooth and cool, but it grows warm and the warmth enters her ear, she is overcome by a wondrous feeling, there in the dark night with the warmth in her ear. She moves her hand to indicate that he should go on speaking, but since she is thinking of the warmth in her ear she does not understand anything. She shakes her head, shakes the warmth from her ear, now hears clearly the word "angel," sees the brightness receding and hears someone moving like one who bears a secret. She sits on the bed and draws the bearskin around her. What did Volmar want? Or was it not he? She presses her eyelids against her eyeballs and sees Richardis in a white dress, faceless. Then she weeps without knowing why, and weeps until the bell rings for Matins.

We sleep too little, she thought on her way to the chapel, we eat too poorly, we have too little exercise and fresh air, but then she saw the well-rested faces of the others, Richardis's brows looked as if they had been drawn with a sharp pencil, Volmar's gestures were very thoughtful, and she felt doubts about what had happened in the night with the angel. I have ransomed your life everywhere you go. They shall be radiant over the grain, the wine, and the oil, and over the young of the flock and the herd; their life shall become like a watered garden, and they shall never languish again. I have ransomed your life everywhere.[8]

[8] Jeremiah 31:11-12.

After Prime, Hildegard wanted to walk over the fields to
the brook with the sisters, taking them all by the hand; wind,
sun, dew, and water would do them good. August is like a
mighty ruler who governs his whole realm in the fullness of
his power. Joy streams forth from it. But Wineldis, Teresa,
and Bertha wanted to prepare the meals, Mechthild has
planned the singing practice, Abilgard wanted this, Ortrud
that, and Clementia and Donata were already in the ointment
kitchen. The time between Prime and Terce is highly coveted.
So Hildegard asked Volmar, and he went with her. I have
ransomed your life everywhere you go. They shall be radiant over the grain, the wine, and the oil, and over the young
of the flock and the herd; their life shall become like a watered
garden, and they shall never languish again.

He opens the door, swings it back, and the morning light
floods in. Hildegard takes her sandals in her hand and tucks
up her shirt so that her shins are bare and the damp grass
can court them. Now I am still shorter, but that doesn't matter. She fastens her sandals to her belt, so that her hands are
free, plucks a head of grain, pulls out the hairs and crushes
the grains. In two weeks we can cut it; it will be a fairly good
harvest. August is really a potentate; see how it ripens the
hemp. We will need that in the herb kitchen; besides that,
we will try to make cloths out of its fibers, to place over
wounds; it may have some healing power. Then Hildegard
is silent, testing this and that, smelling, tasting, crushing,
smelling and tasting again, plucking the things she wants to
bring back to Clementia.

They come to the brook. Hildegard sits down on the bank
and places her feet in the water. Come, she says, the water
does you good, but Volmar is sitting on a stone and wiping
his forehead with his sleeve, although it is not at all hot yet.
Can you skip stones on the water? Hildegard hands him a
bit of white gravel. Volmar throws it, but the stone sinks. Try
it with a flat slate. Volmar throws, and the stone really does
hop: once, twice, three times, then it sinks and a lovely ring
flows outward from it. Hildegard cannot help clapping her

hands. Then she lies flat on her stomach, drinks some of the water, scrambles clumsily up again and brings Volmar the water that still lies in her hand. I have ransomed your life everywhere you go. What is that, a wart on your chin? I never saw that before. She pulls out two little gray hairs, gathers some saliva, makes a foam of it, puts some on her index finger and rubs the finger over the wart, then takes some new saliva and repeats the procedure. Volmar does not resist. Has she gone crazy? In her ointment kitchen there is a piece of silver nitrate that removes warts. I will get some more water and wash your face. But Volmar is already standing; he points to the height of the sun and goes before her with long strides. Hildegard has to put on her sandals to catch up with him; her feet slide in the sandals and she cannot thrust her hands into her sleeves, since she does not want to crush the things she has plucked. Volmar is already standing at the gate, holding it open. He makes a broad, swinging movement and a bow, lets Hildegard enter before him, closes the gate and gives her the key. Surely a wart cannot disappear that fast.

We still have time; I have thought of the final chapter about stones, will you write it down?

> The other stones that arise in different types of earth and in different regions, and that draw from the earth in which they arise different characteristics and different colors, have no great value as instruments of healing—for example marble, sandstone, limestone, tuff, fieldstone, and such. This is either because there is too much moisture in them and it is not balanced by a proper dryness, or because there is too much dryness in them that is not tempered by a proper moisture.[9]

And Volmar writes, repeats, corrects, and reads everything in the complete context. The trees and the stones, thinks Hildegard, Volmar really does have clipped ears. The last stone remains for the crane, when it guards the flocks all night in every place, wherever you go.

[9] *Steine,* 78.

Where
would be the human being
who
could ever
get to the bottom
of things?

IX

The Date Palm

The date palm is warm, moist and tough. It is an image of
bliss. The green leaves of the date palm must be dried in the
sun and ground into powder. This powder, mixed with some
light salt and eaten frequently with bread, is a preventative
against internal decay. The boiled fruit gives the body as much
strength as bread.[1]

A stiffness in the back, a lack of concentration. No pilgrim
brings us dates, and certainly not the green leaves, thinks
Hildegard, and Volmar notices that something is not right;
he pretends that he has to write a finished version of various
things and closes the curtain of the visitor's window. What
is wrong with Irmentraut? She fasted and mortified her flesh
for a year after Hildegard sent her back to her parents; for
the last two years she has been in the convent again, this time
not at her parents' wish, but at her own request. *Nec ego te
condemnabo,*[2] but I should not have readmitted her. One should
not put oneself in danger and climb a high mountain in order
not to sink into the depths later on. She is decaying inside,
her soul has been plundered. "Show me the one whom my
soul loves. Tell me where you pasture your flock, where you
make it lie down at noon, that I may not begin to stray among
the flocks of your companions!"[3] A lack of concentration, a
stiff back.

> The creation would be altogether darkened if it were to de-
> sire to withdraw from any sort of obligation laid on it by God;
> but it has its proper bloom so long as it fulfills its duties with
> a proper commitment. Only in this way does life remain re-
> sponsible in every situation, and a good reputation is gained,
> because all needs are well considered and are satisfied in
> proper order.[4]

[1] *Naturkunde,* 70.
[2] Neither do I condemn you.
[3] Song of Songs 1:7.
[4] *LVM,* 238.

To withdraw from any sort of obligation laid on it by God. To fulfill one's duties. Responsible life. A dark creation. I should not have readmitted her. Mechthild and Ortrud say that she is always the first one at Matins, she fasts more than the others, she is more diligent than any other sister. She keeps all the rules. But she is decaying; her skin keeps breaking out, her soul is plundered, she does not weep; when she says anything at all she speaks in clichés. God's behest, but no half-truths; I should have had it out with her. The bell rings for Vespers. Plectrum, plectrum, shuddering flanks.

O vos angeli, qui custoditis populos! Qui loculum antiqui cordis in fonte aspicitis. O angelus perditus qui volare voluit![5]

During the meal, she has Irmentraut read the text from Proverbs:

A capable wife who can find? She is far more precious than jewels. The heart of her husband trusts in her, and he will have no lack of gain. She does him good, and not harm, all the days of her life. She seeks wool and flax, and works with willing hands. She is like the ships of the merchant, she brings her food from far away. She rises while it is still night and provides food for her household. She considers a field and buys it; with the fruit of her hands she plants a vineyard. She girds herself with strength, and makes her arms strong. She perceives that her merchandise is profitable. Her lamp does not go out at night. She puts her arms to the distaff, and her hands hold the spindle. She opens her hand to the poor, and reaches out her hands to the needy. She is not afraid for her household when it snows, for all her household are clothed in wool. She makes herself coverings; her clothing is fine linen and purple. Her husband is known in the city gates, taking his seat among the elders of the land. She makes linen garments and sells them; she supplies the merchant with sashes.

[5] O you angels who guard the peoples! who behold in the fountain the little place of the ancient heart. O lost angel who wished to fly! *Symphonia* IV. 30. 1-2, 18-19; IV. 29. 14-15.

Strength and dignity are her clothing, and she laughs at the time to come. She opens her mouth with wisdom, and the teaching of kindness is on her tongue. She looks well to the ways of her household, and does not eat the bread of idleness. Her children rise up and call her happy; her husband too, and he praises her.''[6]

Irmentraut's voice was choked; she ran out, and Mechthild read the last part. Everyone has his or her own calling. Mistakes have to be corrected. Hildegard said the closing prayer and followed Irmentraut. She sat beside her until the bell rang for the third time and the sky was beginning to tint itself with green. She had seen it shining, the *lumen corporis*[7] that corresponds to that other light; she had seen it flame up and extinguish itself.

Be sad, oh earth, my garment is torn. Shudder, abyss, my shoes are blackened. A feather without plumage, a skeleton feather. Something that has been shot. Be sad, oh earth, my garment is torn. Shudder, abyss, my shoes are blackened. No pilgrim brings us the fruits and leaves of the tree of bliss, that we could eat with a little light salt. Our shoes are blackened.[8]

[6] Proverbs 31:10-28.

[7] Light of the body (cf. Matthew 6:22).

[8] See Hildegard's letter to Werner of Kirchheim, ca. 1170 or 1171. A translation may be found in Hildegard of Bingen, *Mystical Writings,* ed. by Fiona Bowie and Oliver Davies, with new translations by Robert Carver (New York: Crossroad, 1990) 141–43.

The Willow

Be sad, oh earth, shudder, abyss, my garment is torn, my shoes are blackened. But Hildegard was not sickened by Irmentraut's death. After the burial in the convent cemetery, she was all the more concerned for the sisters, taking care that Donata's complexion did not grow pale, that Clementia got a long-legged stool, helped Alfriede with the apple peeling, held the band on which the pieces of apple were arranged, cleaned the chickens for Wineldis and roasted the hearts, bandaged Teresa's burned hand, massaged Mechthild's swollen feet, devoted more time to the sick people who came to the gate, listening longer and more carefully, more patiently. In the time between Vespers and Compline she sang with the sisters, and she herself rang the bell for evening prayer. The people returning from the fields heard it and were glad: Listen, Hildegard herself is ringing. Then Alma was standing before the gate, with ulcers on her face, hands, arms, breast and legs, staring vacantly; Hildegard smelled the stink.

> People who have sexual intercourse with animals, thus degrading their noble human nature with such despicable shame, but then later become penitent over this dastardly fault, should submit to a penance for their guilt: they are to be punished with the strictest fasting and the most severe caning. They should also, from that time forward, avoid the type of animal with which they have sinned, in order that their penitential mood may give annoyance to the devil.[9]

Be sad, oh abyss, my shoes are blackened. Hildegard shoved Alma into the guests' bathhouse, took off her mourning clothes, told her to get into the tub, and washed her body and her hair. *O vos angelis, qui custoditis populos!*[10] She made her get into fresh water a second time. What prayers do you know? None. Do you know how to pray? No. Didn't you learn how? No. Where are your parents? Don't know. The servant boy beats me, the servant girls beat me, the horses and cows kick me. Only the nanny goats. Pus and blood, burns and pain, the servant beats her with willow switches. Hildegard rubs ointment on her body, then puts a clean shirt on her. She cannot comb her hair, so she cuts it short. Beaten with wil-

[9] *LVM*, 177.
[10] O you angels who guard the peoples!

low wands, kicked by billy goats. Take this and drink! The others have been asleep a long time.

The next morning after Prime, Hildegard rides to Alma's master and mistress. The brother goes with her the whole way. I could just as well have walked, my back hurts. *O virga ac diadema purpurae Regis, quae es in clausura tua sicut lorica.*[11] The master and mistress are not lords and ladies, but big-boned people with callused hands and dull faces; there is syrup in the man's beard. Workers are scarce, but nobody refuses Hildegard anything. She does not ask even for a glass of water, does not look at the servant or the billy goat. By Sext she has returned, her back stiff; she can still smell the filth, the syrup in the man's beard and on the dogs' backs. I am cast down in the haunt of the jackals, my mouth is dried up like a potsherd.[12] She chews the watered wine, softens her bread, listens to the reading: when they had gone ashore, they saw a charcoal fire there, with fish on it, and bread. A hundred fifty-three great fish. Come and eat. Kicked by billy goats, beaten with willow switches. A charcoal fire is lighted. A hundred fifty-three great fish.[13]

After dinner, a delegation of sisters asks that Alma be removed from the guest house. I should send you all to the lepers for a while, thinks Hildegard, but she only says that the decision is hers and that she has decided to keep Alma until she is healed. She speaks softly and without repetition.

Volmar also warns Hildegard. Send her to St. Disibod, they will perform an exorcism there, there is no other way. Just write, says Hildegard, it is only a short text:

> The willow is cold. It is an image of vice. For human beings it is of little value; one can use it only for a few external things. The box tree is dry, still warmer than the syben tree and there-

---

[11] O branch and diadem of the king's purple, you who are in your enclosure like a breastplate. *Symphonia* II.20. 1a ("O virga ac diadema").
[12] Psalms 44:19; 22:15.
[13] Cf. John 21:9-11.

fore, like it, is green all year. Anyone with a bodily rash should grind the bark and leaves of this tree and press out the juice, mix it with some licorice, heat the whole mixture in pure wine and drink it warm, many times over. This will keep the pain and poison of the rash on the surface of the body and prevent it from penetrating within. In addition, the same juice should be mixed with some palm oil and, with a feather, rings should be traced around the rash with this mixture. If this is done frequently, it will be healed. But one must take care always to drink first; otherwise the salve that is rubbed on the skin will drive the decay into the body instead of drawing it out. Like the sap of the tree, its wood is also strong and has healing power.[14]

Volmar repeats, makes no correction, reads the whole again. Add one more sentence to the rest of the text:

O human, see then the human being rightly: the human being has heaven and earth and the whole creation in itself, and yet is a complete form, and in it everything is already present, though hidden.[15]

She speaks more slowly than usual, enunciates each part of the sentence separately, every word, then repeats the whole. This evening after Compline she will bathe Alma again, anoint her, give her to drink, teach her the first phrase of the Our Father, the lovely word "heaven" and the gentle relative clause. Alma will work her lips, her teeth, her tongue. And so it will continue, every evening. And the stink will disappear, the wounds will heal. The human being has heaven and earth and the whole creation within itself, and yet is a complete form, in which everything is already present, though hidden. No billy goats' kicks, no blows with willow wands. *O vos angeli.*

Alas for hope. Shrieks are heard outside; Hildegard rushes out. Alma is rolling among the pigs; she has torn the clothes

[14] *Naturkunde,* 74, 71.
[15] *Heilkunde,* 50.

from her body, she is lusting, barking, grunting; the swine's snouts are in her vagina and anus; she is surrounded by snuffling, sniffing hordes, licked, stepped on, pulled by her hair, tossed about; climbing, falling bodies, shrill cries. The swineherd and a brother come running; they throw the animals aside, beat them with sticks, kick them, Alma flings them away from her with blows and kicks, bawling, whimpering, roaring, bleeding within and without. Finally she is subdued; the shepherd strikes her hard in the face and the men bind her hands behind her back, tie her feet together, throw a blanket over her, tie it with cords, and drag the bundle into the house.

Hildegard leaves Alma lying on the floor, tied up as she is, and sends the men away. She sits down beside her. The girl tears at the cords with her teeth, rears up, rolls herself into a ball, howls, shrieks, spits around her. Hildegard sits there for an hour, two hours, does not hear the bell, only sits there until Alma is exhausted. Then she unties the cords from the blanket, from her feet and hands, lays her feet together, her hands right and left alongside her body, the head on her own thigh, spreads a sheet on the body, wipes the sweat from her brow, the blood from her eyes. Her eyelashes twitch as if under electric blows, her nose flares, her muscles flutter. Beaten with willow wands, kicked by goats and pigs. Be sad, o earth, shudder, abyss, my garment is torn, my shoes are blackened.

When the bell rings for Matins, Hildegard lifts Alma's head from her lap, stumbles to the chapel. Her voice is hoarse, her fingernails broken, her habit stinking and smeared with blood. Stares from all sides. What if Alma wakes up? How do you do an exorcism? Get help from St. Disibod. Volmar. Restore peace to the house. From my confinement, lead me into open space. The sun will not harm you by day nor the moon by night. Only my shoes are blackened.

And then the wind arose, a warm October wind, too late to strike the leaves from the trees, too early to bring snow. Hildegard's enemy. A wind from the north. She sets herself against it, holds her ears closed, draws her veil across her face, breathes in defensive puffs, senses numbness behind her forehead, two fists at the back of her skull, stiffness in her back. Exorcism in this condition?

Repeat after me: "Our Father," only two words, say them, work your tongue, your lips, your gums; but Alma licked her lips and spit out the words. She will run to the pigs again soon; the men will beat and bind her. The lovely word "heaven," and the gentle relative clause. The October wind ate into Hildegard's innards and took a firm hold. She saw, on a stage without a background, a human form with open arms, covered everywhere with eyes. Mist drifted over the figure and rendered it invisible. Repeat after me. Alma tore her face with her fingernails until the ulcers broke and the blood flowed; she drove her nails through her face again, licked the blood, spat it at Hildegard, then ran outside and vomited.

Volmar summoned two monks from St. Disibod, and the three of them undertook the exorcism. Hildegard sat there, watching to make sure that the men did not become violent, admonishing them to patience and kindness. The process lasted three days; Alma was bound hand and foot and given no nourishment except water, and for an hour at a time, in alternation, she was subjected to the ritual and then left to rest. She struggled, screamed, spat, vomited, menstruated; her eyes and tongue started from her head, she bit out her teeth, her fingernails and toenails split. And Hildegard sat there, soiled from head to foot.

On the third day Alma was quieter; her ulcers closed, the scabs fell off, her face and body returned to their proper form. The men untied her. Beaten with willow wands, kicked by pigs and billy goats.

Hildegard lay down, stiff and silent. October wind from the north. Be sad, o earth, shudder, abyss.

Linden and Beech

Lie down, stretch out, the earth opens, take your arms with you, your feet, let your eyeballs sink into your head, your skin clings to your cheekbones, your tongue is stiff, your ears harden, the flesh on your hips and legs is decomposing, the bearskin is made of lead. Far away the bell rings; the strokes are thin and far. Don't let the wind come in, cover up the stars. Lie down, stretch out. They are washing you, changing the sheets, spooning something into you. Let me sleep. My will is crushed.

God, the mighty thinker, the artist, the skillful handworker who sets the glowing artifact under the bellows, turns and turns it until it has been completely perfected. Do not treat me as a stranger and root me out of the land of the living, a portion and cup are mine.

Richardis is with her during the night, forty nights long, kneeling beside the bed, making the bearskin light. She lays her head beside Hildegard, breathing, until, after forty days, her sister moves her toes, twists her feet, traces Richardis's eyebrows with her index finger, sits up, sways so that others must hold her, breathes deeply, brings her eyes back from within her head, with her tongue pushes her lips free of her teeth, smoothes both of Richardis's eyebrows with her index fingers. Mirror of the moon's path. She smiles. Do not root me out of the land of the living, a stranger. She asks for a sip of wine, drinks, breathes. She lays her brow against Richardis's brow. Green feathered with brown. She stands up, swaying so that the others must hold her, walks, takes the sheet down from the window. The wind has died. Yes, Richardis says, it has grown cold.

You have turned my mourning into dancing, you have taken off my sackcloth and clothed me with joy, set my feet in a broad place.[16] Hildegard hears the sisters' song of jubi-

[16] Psalms 30:11; 31:8.

lation. Set your feet in a broad place, clothed with joy. Volmar has cut a staff for her from chestnut wood. Strengthening of the veins and all the powers. She walks, supported by the staff and by Volmar, in the garden that is white with frost. She looks up at the linden tree, lays a hand on its trunk. Fragile, because it is too warm. Do you think that a date palm could grow here? No, you need not try it, Volmar says quietly, and Hildegard nods, places a hand around the willow branch. Look, it is already budding. It is well for her with Volmar at her side, and with the staff that grows warm in her hand. The beech tree, she says: moderation, that's it; moderation, and care for life. The air has done her good, but now she must go back into the house. She smells the staff.

> The linden is very warm. All its warmth is located in the roots and from there rises into the branches and leaves. The linden is the image of fragility. Against heart problems it is helpful to eat frequently with one's bread a powder made from the interior of its roots. In summer, when one goes to sleep, one should cover the eyes and the whole face with fresh linden leaves. This makes the eyes pure and clear.[17]

It is good to sit here, looking at Volmar's big ear, letting the words come, hearing his voice when he repeats the text.

> The beech has an equal amount of warmth and coldness; that is its proper measure. It is an image of discipline. When the beech leaves begin to appear, but are not yet completely out, go to a beech, grasp a twig in your left hand, hold it over your right shoulder and say: I cut off your greenness in order that, through the living word, you may heal all the juices in the human being that have taken the wrong path or have changed themselves into false, yellow gall. While saying these words, hold the twig in the left hand, cut it with an iron knife, and keep it until the cycle of the year has come to a close. Do this every year. And if anyone is suffering from jaundice, cut off a piece of the twig, put it in a bowl, pour some wine

[17] *Naturkunde,* 72.

over it and for three days give it warm to the sick person to drink. If the person takes it fasting, and you call on God at the same time, he or she will get well, if God does not will otherwise.[18]

Shouldn't we include melancholia along with yellow gall, asked Volmar. No, that is superfluous. Just the moss now, and that will be enough for today; I still have to practice walking.

> When the trees grow old or begin to lose their internal freshness, or when young trees by some accident are internally weakened, they extrude the freshness and health that they should have within them onto their bark. Thus moss grows on the bark. Some mosses on certain trees have healing power; others, growing on decayed trees, have almost no such power. The moss that grows on pear and apple trees and on beeches can be used as a poultice against gout. But first it must be boiled and the water must be squeezed out of it.[19]

Volmar wrote slowly, leaving Hildegard plenty of time. What are decayed trees, what does "certain trees" mean, he asked. Just write it; we can always make it more precise later. He looked up, and their glances locked. And she loved him very much. I am really still very weak, she thought.

Hildegard practiced sitting and walking, speaking and singing, and one day after dinner she said: we have a trunk full of white silk; we will make clothes for ourselves out of that. Let us begin by taking our measurements today. The sisters looked uncertainly at one another. What is this? What does it mean? We have always praised poverty. Silk gleams on the skin and in the eyes. We ought to sell it in Augsburg or Bamberg and buy a vineyard, or a section of river for fishing. We, with our cropped hair, heavy sandals, shapeless bodies? I know what you are thinking, said Hildegard, but I want to see you in these gowns. And so the key to the trunk was brought;

[18] Ibid.
[19] *Naturkunde,* 77.

Richardis unlocked it, Ortrud and Teresa lifted the bales out, removed the sacking, and unfolded several ells of material. Shining purity. Hildegard imagined Richardis: how beautiful you are, my love, how very beautiful; your eyes are doves behind your veil. Your hair is like a flock of goats moving down the slopes of Gilead.[20]

But the gowns were never made. Abilgard and some of the other sisters raised objections, and since Hildegard would not give in they agreed that, instead of gowns, they would make floor-length veils to wear on feast days. Moderation, thought Hildegard, the skin is a sensitive organ.

The veils were ready by Epiphany. The young sisters rushed into the bath house to wash their hair and curl it a little on their foreheads. The veil slid smoothly over Richardis. Your cheeks are like halves of a pomegranate behind your veil.[21] Lovely child. Hildegard had to laugh at her own self, she looked so comical.

Then you shall see and be radiant; your heart shall thrill and rejoice, because the abundance of the sea shall be brought to you . . . a multitude of camels shall cover you, the young camels of Midian and Epha, all those from Sheba shall come. They shall bring gold and frankincense, and shall proclaim the praise of the Lord. You shall see and be radiant.[22]

But in the night Hildegard had a nightmare. She was looking for a flower for Richardis's hair, and when she finally found a red hibiscus bloom and was about to stick it in her hair, the hair caught fire, and Richardis ran away, blazing and screaming. And the bridegroom outside the window, just ready to embrace the bride, disappeared. Hildegard awakened, shook the image from her eyes, the scream from her ears, tried to recapture her joy, saw the dromedaries, the camels, Midian and Epha and Sheba; how beautiful you are, my love, your hair is like a flock of goats moving down the

[20] Song of Songs 4:1.
[21] Song of Songs 4:3.
[22] Isaiah 60: 4-6. (Matins, Office for Epiphany).

slopes of Gilead. Your heart shall thrill and rejoice, because the abundance of the sea shall be brought to you. Weeping shall be changed into joy, put off your garments of mourning, gird yourself with joy, set your feet in a broad place, you shall see and rejoice. When summer comes, we will make wreaths of beech leaves; I will plait linden leaves into mine.

Beech and linden,
the willow
and the date palm.

Discipline and
fragility,
vice and death
instead of bliss.

My garment is torn,
I put off the garments of mourning,
put off
the shoes that are soiled,
set my feet in freedom.

Floods of young camels
bring from Epha and Sheba
silk and a chestnut staff.

X

The Soldier

Hildegard, Richardis, and Volmar worked in an even rhythm. Hildegard dictated, Volmar wrote and revised, Richardis wrote out the edited version. Each was concentrated, and at the same time alert to the others. The two voices alternated, Richardis wrote silently.

> The fern is warm and dry and also has a moderate share of sap. The devil flees this plant, and it has certain powers that are reminiscent of the sun, since, like the sun, it lights up the darkness. It banishes phantoms, and therefore the evil spirits dislike it. In the places where it grows, the devil does not practice his illusions, and it avoids and detests the places and the house where the devil is. Lightning, thunder and hail seldom fall there, and it rarely rains on the field where the fern grows. Anyone who carries fern branches is safe against the snares of the evil one and against assaults on life and limb. Against deafness, a small bag containing fern seeds may be placed in the ear. If someone cannot speak properly, he or she should place fern seed under the tongue, and will then be able to speak. Those with a weak memory and little understanding should carry fern seed in the hand to strengthen them.[1]

Hildegard asked for a short pause, closed her eyes, pressed thumb and middle finger against the base of her nose. Someone was twisting in the throes of death, falling asleep, rearing up again, sighing, calling her name, groaning, collapsing. Hildegard saw a face twisted with pain, a writhing figure, straw and sheets tossed about, rolling eyes. They will lay hands on the sick and they will be healed. She placed her hand on the man's forehead. Be healed. The form vanished from her eyes. She saw Richardis and Volmar writing, still heard the sighing and groaning, then a lighter breathing. I forgot one part, you can insert it in the middle, after "life and limb."

[1] *Naturkunde,* 26. See *Medicine,* 111.

Just as there is within human beings a sense of good and evil, so also good and bad herbs are made for them. The juice of the fern, however, is directed to the good, and that is why everything evil and magical flees before it; hence it does not permit the effects of poison and sorcery to enter into a house. The fresh leaves, bound over the eyes, make them clear and drive out anything that darkens them. [2]

A few weeks later, a soldier stood at the gate of the convent and asked to speak to Hildegard. He said he would wait until she returned from Eibingen; he split wood in the courtyard until there was no more to split, he sawed, chopped and split some more until it was all ready for use, he stacked, leveled, swept until the court was clean. And Hildegard came, but the soldier had nothing to say and stood stiff as a pole. She stretched herself tall and took his head in her two hands: now be really healed, in your soul also. She saw the dots of happiness spring up in his eyes. He swayed, and—Lord, my God. I am healthy and alive.

That evening, Hildegard fell asleep earlier than usual. The day was past, she lay down, pulled the bearskin up to her chin, asked herself why everyone is so anxious to live and not to die, and fell asleep. She took fern seed from her ears and from beneath her tongue and scattered it over the field. *Benedicite montes et colles.* [3]

[2] *Naturkunde,* 26.
[3] Bless, mountains and hills.

Branches and boxes,
hell to the left,
the world to the right,
over all
heaven, round and high.

Close your eyes,
throw the stone,
hop on one leg
from the box to the world,
back to the branch,
into hell,
and only your leg holds you up.

The one who falls
must begin again from the beginning,
close your eyes,
throw the stone
straight into heaven.

XI

The Altar Cloth

When the children at Bermersheim played this game, Hildegard always lost. You have to hold your breath until you are dizzy; then you think you are floating, and it is really easy, said Odilia, but Hildegard did not want to. Clementia could make short throws, touch the stone with her foot, push it farther and get right into "heaven"; Hildegard could not. Why not hop with both feet at the same time? Why throw a blind stone before you? She stood and admired the sisters: with my eyes closed I will never get anywhere; and she would have liked so much to sit still in "heaven," looking down the ladder from above, at "hell" and the "world." But then Ludger brought her a fern seedling from the forest, or gave her a branch of rue whose warmth, he said, would soothe overexcited emotions, and he showed her how to prepare and fertilize the ground, how to plant and prune.

And Hildegard stood and admired her plants, encouraged them, made declarations of love to them, egged them on to greater beauty, deeper greenness, praised the sun, too, and the rain and the air that cooked these greening bodies and ripened them. And when the fern unrolled a leaf before her very eyes she shouted aloud, put her ear to it, licked it with her tongue, forgot to admire Clementia's cabbage heads and exclaim over Odilia's fine flowers, called Ludger, and he lifted her high, the child, the feather, high in the air, and turned in a circle so that heaven and garden were a great wheel with Ludger in the middle, a wheel that swung around, weaving everything together and lifting Hildegard up inside it. Green light, that is life.

Each child had a plot of its own, and each could do with it what it liked; no one was allowed to talk anyone else into anything, but if a bed deteriorated and became overgrown with weeds it would be taken away. Once, when Hildegard had been sick for a long time, she kept her plot from being taken away by building a stable in it, and a house and a church, and setting up a wall all around it. Sometimes Ludger knelt beside her: knead the clay till it is softer, use stones and braces to hold everything fast, make a practical plan: don't put the bake house on the south and the sheep pen on the north, and don't build the church too high so it cuts off the light from the garden, the garden and the well—if a well has no light, the water will go bad.

A well? You always have to begin with a well, and Ludger dug a deep hole, Hildegard squatted beside him, her hand on his thigh. A well without water? The water from the sky will collect there, only have patience. The well was finished, but no water collected. Hildegard hung a little bell in her church, rang it every day, put her king in front of the church door, set the fairy by the well, rang the bell. You must have a lot more patience, said Ludger. Patience. "She is dressed in a white tunic, the folds of which cast pale green shadows, on her head she wears a three-pointed crown, shining red like sparkling hyacinth."[1]

Patience and the altar cloth. Jutta had brought linen from the chest and bright thread; sketches were made on a board and then transferred to the cloth, stitch by stitch. The table and the room were much too small for the cloth; it had to be folded and unfolded and pleated again, and new things were sketched and copied on it, stitch by stitch, dot by dot, from the end of the cloth to the middle, and then the whole repeated again from the other end. They were going to do some building at St. Disibod, a new wing to the cloister, an expansion of the women's enclosure, a bake house, a stable and a great church with a new altar. The cornerstone had been laid: the women could see it through the grill and the open door of the chapel, through which they glimpsed a spotless sky and sun-warmed air full of tenderness rushed in, so that Hildegard lifted her arms high, gathering and embracing the air.

[1] *Scivias* III. 3 (*HB*, 344).

Abbot Burkhard and the monks had thrown back their hoods, a great many people were there, people from the neighborhood, people from Cologne and Mainz with brilliant robes and sparkling chains around their necks. And one man who looked like Ludger lifted up the dirt with a graceful swing, and Abbot Burkhard held the stone, while the prior stood nearby holding the reliquary, and both of them knelt and laid the reliquary and the stone in the earth. Before Hildegard's eyes, the stone shot up into the sky, not like a column, but as a mighty cornerstone, shining white in the sun. Everyone sang, and the women joined in, and Burkhard nodded genially, still a little breathless from the weight of the stone and the excitement of the moment. A foundation stone. Now the work could begin.

In the night, Ludger digs a deep hole. Hildegard has her hand on his thigh and she is singing, but then she is supposed to bring stones for the well, and she drags a heavy stone, bigger than she is, takes it on her right, then her left shoulder, on her arm, on her back. But she does not approach Ludger; instead, she draws farther and farther away from him, stops, tries to turn around, to call to him, to set the stone down, but she is out of breath, she drags it farther, finds herself in a wasteland, and the stone is growing, she swings the stone onto her back again, it breaks into fragments and she stands among the broken pieces and shrieks so that Jutta comes and shakes her awake, wipes the sweat from her forehead and prays softly, so softly that Hildegard cannot understand the words and so cannot join in and only takes care that her hands are safely laid in Jutta's hands, and she falls asleep again, and Ludger changes into Abbot Burkhard and doesn't puff any more at all.

When, in the time afterward, the noises of building begin every day after Prime, mixed with the voices of the builders—more to the left, slower, more to the right, lower, forward, stop, go on—Hildegard could not hear enough of the words, so space-spanning and full of motion. I wish I could stand there and watch, observe closely, help them: knead the clay until it is both malleable and stiff, load it on the wagon, stroke the ox's neck so that it will pull the wagon, and spread the clay on the stone, lay another stone on that stone, press the clay into the cracks and smooth it so that clay and stone become one. And she saw how the church was growing.

But she sat with Jutta and little Jutta, whom they called Jona, working on the altar cloth, and she was not very skillful with needle and thread—stitch by stitch, green all around, miles of it. When we get to the branches, then we can make the yellow and red stripes, the brown background, the broad waves of black, red and white stripes around the building, and then we can begin the churches, temple, mosques, towers and synagogues in red, blue, green and yellow, and get closer to the well and the figures. Patience, says Jutta, you must be much more patient. That was a hard test for little girls and a difficult task, almost as difficult as the building outdoors. We need many more hands, says Hildegard, listening to the voices outside and repeating the songs that Jutta sang. She set notes to a psalm verse, spoke a part of a prayer, sat silent and embroidered, saw the bright buildings, embroidered and sang, practiced patience—patience and precision.

During the siesta Hildegard went through the cloister courtyard on tiptoe, set her ear to the wall, looked at the sky for a reflection of what was going on beyond the wall. I will always put a gateway in a wall, a gate that can be opened, a door that can be unlocked with a great key, so that I can see the fields and hills and the church growing and a little more sky, so that the wind can bend my lashes and pull out a hair from under my coif. And the wall must have towers so that people can see far, far away, up to the firmament. But the door must never be walled shut.

The road from Bermersheim to St. Disibod is very long, miles of it, especially the last part near the foot of the mountain, but she pushes the singing wall ahead of her, tirelessly, her cloak is already crumpled, she cannot distinguish Ludger's voice nor Gimbert's, only those of her mother and sisters, until they are lost in the general murmuring. Her cloak rubs against her father's cloak, she walks alone, her hands hidden in the sleeves. You must have a lot more patience, says Ludger. She is dressed in a white tunic, the folds of which cast pale green shadows, on her head she wears a three-pointed crown, shining red like sparkling hyacinth.

There are lights in the distance and the singing of the monks, torn away by the wind. And there stands Jutta, tall and bright, with hands made raw by the cold. Her father bends down to Hildegard, grasps her shoulders; a star shatters on her forehead. After that she hears only the noises of wall building, the dull sounds of stone on stone and the scraping of the trowels that blots out the litanies. Verse for verse, saint for saint, and the stillness with the shattered star. Light green shadows, red-glowing hyacinth.

I will build walls, but I will not forget the doors that can be unlocked with a great key for the wind and the air and the light.

The Well

For the expansion of the women's cloister, the wall had to be opened. Hildegard saw the wagons laden with sand and stones; four oxen had to draw them. She saw their bowed heads and the whips that the yelling drivers cracked over their backs; she was shocked, looked more closely, forgot to pay attention to the expansion of the sky, was uncertain about the tunic and crown of patience. But when she looked at the altar cloth again, drew thread alongside thread, ripped out what she had done because it lacked precision, and tried again, she forgot the whips and listened to the discussion between Abbot Burkhard and Jutta.

A cell whose length, breadth and height are only the measure of a single human being is too small; one must be able to walk back and forth, lift the arms and swing them, jump. And no bars on the windows. Anyone who does not want to stay can freely go. No bars for sun, moon, and stars, and for the wind. And a visitors' window at the end of the corridor, big enough so one can see the eyes, nose and mouth of the visitor.

The ornamental border of the altar cloth was finished. Jona had quick hands, and sometimes Jutta helped, too. We will fill in the empty space later; now we will embroider the black edge around the buildings. Black? Yes, black. It must be so. The cloister was growing, the corridor, four new cells, a workroom, a refectory. Hildegard felt the dryness of the floor, the walls, sensed the warmth of the stones and the clay, and when the workers put the roof on she felt the retreat of the wind, the departure of the light, but not as a loss. Silence. Shelter. The beating of the heart.

You must always begin with the well, Ludger had said; Hildegard repeated it to Abbot Burkhard, and he smiled and made no objection. There is still time. And the well must have light, so that the water does not go bad. Abbot Burkhard nodded. The water of the heavens can collect there. Yes, yes, Burkhard sighed. And in fact, the next day a young man came into the cloister garden and dug the hole for the well. That was hard work, but Hildegard looked admiringly at the colorful dirt from the deeper level, at the strong arms and hands. What is your name? Robert. Robert? How deep must you dig? Until I reach the ground water. Ground water, what a lovely phrase. Robert dug farther, and Hildegard saw that his ears had gone red.

When the shaft had been walled in and the building of the well curb above ground began, the girls were permitted to gather the stones. She dragged in bluish and whitish blocks, and when Robert had spread the clay, she set the stones and pressed them down. Robert had a sharp eye for the thickness

105

of the layers of clay, for the size and shape of the stones, and thus it was a beautiful well, round, with a smooth edge, much larger than the one in Bermersheim, and at midday the light thrust its beams into it. Those were wonderful siestas. The only problem was that the water did not want to come, not from heaven and not from the earth. I should climb in, thought Hildegard, stroked the edge, bent over it and sang a song into the depths.

When the ground water level rises the water will come, said Robert, smoothing the earth around the well. You must only have patience. Please, if you could bring me fern shoots from the forest, said Hildegard. Robert looked at her uncomprehendingly, but the next day he handed her a basket full of fern shoots, and Hildegard planted them. The ferns put down roots and grew, but the water did not come.

The sketch for the altar cloth had a well with three figures.

> Two of them stand in an utterly clear well, which is surrounded and crowned with a round, porous stone. They all seem to be rooted in the well, as trees sometimes appear to grow in water. One figure is surrounded by a purple glow, the second by a blinding white light, while the third figure stands outside the well, on the stone just described, dressed in a gown of blinding white; her figure is gloriously shining.[2]

But Hildegard did not yet know what to call these three figures. And how long would it be before she reached the well with her needle? They were still embroidering the black wall of the world; much too often the threads were not laid closely enough and the gap had to be filled; then the whole thing was too thick and snarled on the underside, and there was nothing to do but to take it all out and begin again from the beginning. O glittering hyacinth in the crown of patience.

Then Hildegard took the mattress from her bed and slept on the board. Cover yourself with clay and become a clay figu-

---

[2] *De operatione Dei* III. 8. 1. (See *Book of Divine Works,* 204).

rine. She was long since awake when Jutta called them to Matins. She stayed after Compline, sunk within herself. She dipped her bread in water. She embroidered black thread after black thread. She scoured the stones in the newly built rooms. She avoided the well. She did not look for Robert. She slept in shivering cold. She was kicked and shoved. She saw in a glittering light the lion with gaping mouth, bursting with pain, the spear in his back, twisting himself; she saw the blackening of his pelt and the dying light in his eyes. Drop a golden ball into a well. Follow the spindle into a well and waken in a pleasant meadow. Sit by a well, shed the old skin, wash yourself, do not put on the old skin again. Pearls need not grow from tears. The throat dry as potsherds. Cast down in the haunt of the jackals. Lay aside the old skin, beside the well.

Jutta was silent. At night she laid a blanket over Hildegard, dried her forehead, held her hand. In the daytime she shortened the hours of embroidery, lengthened the readings, practiced new psalm verses, was silent. And one day, when the autumn rains had begun, Abbot Burkhard came, took Hildegard by the hand and went with her to the well. See and taste. It is quite clear. Holy sobriety! Hildegard wept, but Abbot Burkhard laid his hand on her shoulder: the earth is a living thing, the water seeks its own way. We must simply have patience. And Hildegard was amazed that her weeping was not painful.

Ears

Jutta and Jona, Jona and Jutta, the profiles of the monks under their hoods, once a month Abbot Burkhard, Jutta and Jona, Jona and Jutta. Singing and prayer and silence, a walk to the well, a taste of the water, a stroking of the ferns, silence, prayer, singing, embroidery, the profiles of the monks in their hoods, Jona and Jutta. And then an hour between

Prime and Terce, an hour between None and Vespers: Volmar. I will work with you, the grill won't bother us, we will imagine it away, there is a lot to do. And if you have any worries, you can tell me those, too, through the grill that isn't there.

And he shook the hood from his head: what a big ear! He turned his head, and the other ear was just as big: Hildegard was struck dumb with amazement, kissed the ear and, when Volmar turned his head, kissed the other ear. I will pull myself up by these ears when I don't know how to go on, and she laid her hands on Volmar's ears, and he stood up, much taller than a tree, and lifted her up. *Hodie si vocem audieritis, nolite obdurare corda vestra: sicut in exacerbatione secundum diem tentationis in deserto: ubi tentaverunt me patres vestri, probaverunt, et viderunt opera mea.* [3]

She had many strange words to learn. Volmar questioned her, corrected, had her repeat and corrected again. *Probaverunt et viderunt opera mea.* [4] And many words that she had often spoken she now began to understand: the world was doubly full of names, deeds and sufferings.

> When the ears receive the sound of each and every phenomenon, everything, whatever and wherever it is, can be recognized according to its essence. For this reason the human being seeks to discover that essence, and still more its spirit. The soul's power thus to sense through the ears, even when hearing can yield nothing more, is not thus made superfluous and is in no way sated; rather it longs to know and understand much more. Hearing is, in fact, the beginning of the rational soul. [5]

Volmar was a good and lasting providence; Hildegard, hanging on his ears, did not sink, even when all her strength threatened to leave her.

[3] Today, if you should hear the voice, harden not your hearts, as on the day of temptation in the wilderness: when your ancestors tested me, and put me to the proof, though they had seen my works (Psalm 95: 8-9).

[4] They put me to the proof, though they had seen my works.

[5] *De operatione Dei* IV. 39.

108

Changes happening because of Volmar and the hours of learning, changes through the coming of more girls who occupied the new cells. Distribution of tasks, getting attuned to one another. Jutta sometimes looked tired. But the work on the altar cloth was more and more visible. Hildegard had left the world to the others and begun on the well; she had even sketched water flowing from the sides of the well toward the world. And the singing was stronger, Hiltrud and Mechthild had clear, bright voices, Margarethe's added a darker note. The result was a magnificent *Gloria Patri,* the strophes and counter-strophes emerged more clearly, and sometimes Abbot Burkhard smiled across at them, which inspired them to still more intensive practice and rehearsals. Hildegard thought less often of the star that had shattered on her forehead.

Hildegard and Hiltrud are in the garden gathering onions: they must pull them out of the earth, cut off the tops, clean the bulbs. Hiltrud's knife slips and cuts her finger; blood flows. Hildegard takes the finger in her mouth; she tastes sand, onion and blood; she sucks, wraps her tongue around the finger, ties it up in her handkerchief. They go on working; soon they are finished. Look, there is no blood on the cloth, says Hiltrud; the wound has closed, you can't even see it. Your saliva has healing power.

All saliva has healing power, says Hildegard, but that isn't it. The vessel has closed itself; all I did was to lick the blood away. You needn't say anything to Jutta about it. They take hands and run to the well and see two faces in the water and each scoops a handful, each gives it to the other, and she drinks. And they run back to their onions that have such a winey juice. "They grow from the wind and the moisture of the ground. And of all the plants of the leek family they are the least harmful, because they do not excite the juices."[6] And before Hiltrud picks up her basket she pushes back Hildegard's coif and whispers something in her ear, the beginning of the

[6] *Naturkunde,* 34.

rational soul, and Hildegard nods and still tastes the blood, with sand and onions.

In the night Hildegard goes with Robert through a fernwood. Sometimes he catches her around the hips and carries her a little way in front of him, then again he moves before her, and she cannot follow him. The seeds hop from the leaves into their ears, but do not reach their tongues, and then Robert is gone, and Hildegard is lost in the fern fronds that unroll and grasp at her; she cannot go on. The bell for Matins rings shrilly.

> He sends out his command to the earth; his word runs swiftly.
> He gives snow like wool, he scatters frost like ashes.
> He hurls down hail like crumbs; who can stand before his cold?
> He sends out his word and melts them; he makes his wind blow,
> and the waters flow.[7]

I will give you a concept, said Volmar, and you find the opposite: *injusticia, inobedientia,* and *infidelitas* are easy; all you have to do is drop the prefix. There are more such pairs, but what will you set opposite torpor? That means tedium. Hildegard considered. *Beatitudo* perhaps, or *sanctitas* or *caeleste desiderium,* the desire for heavenly things. But Volmar shook his head and said *"fortitudo,"* and then Hildegard shook her head: rather *"misericordia"* or *"caritas."* We will work it out, it is a mighty world of light and dark; try to tell me what *"caritas"* is.[8] But Hildegard was silent, looking at Volmar; the bar ran between his eyes and eyebrows. I will read it to you: "Love is patient (*caritas patiens est*); love is kind; love is not envious or boastful or arrogant or rude. It does not insist on its own way; it is not irritable or resentful; it does not rejoice

---

[7] Psalm 147:15-18.

[8] Injustice . . . disobedience . . . infidelity . . . blessedness . . . sanctity . . . fortitude . . . mercy . . . love.

in wrongdoing, but rejoices in the truth. It bears all things, believes all things, hopes all things, endures all things."[9] I must write that down and think it through, said Hildegard, it is all lovely and good.

She brought her mouth close to the grill, and Volmar shook his hood down and held his ear close: one of the figures on the well is love, perhaps the one with the purple glow, she said, "I, love, am the glory of God, the living God. All creation is reflected in me. My radiance reveals the form of things."[10] She had whispered it as if it was meant only for Volmar. "All creation," do you understand? And Volmar nodded and drew his hood up again over his head. We will talk it all over, we have time, and Hildegard thought, I will pull myself up by those ears when I don't know how to go on, and Hiltrud will support me, as she promised; I am quite sure that love is the glory of the living God and that all being is reflected in it, even if I should be set on high pinnacles. *Probaverunt et viderunt opera mea.* Snow like wool, frost like ashes, ice like stones, frozen water. He sends forth his word, the waters run. Look, whispered Hiltrud, the cut is not visible. And Hildegard nodded, but her heart did not leap in her breast.

[9] 1 Corinthians 13: 4-7.
[10] *De operatione Dei* III. 8. 2. (See *Book of Divine Works*, 204, 206).

*Caritas
patiens
est.*

XII

Owl and Screech Owl

When the ears receive the sound of every phenomenon, everything in nature can be recognized according to its essence.[1]

Hildegard sometimes heard the whispering, hissing and moaning of the owls and, farther off, the "ku-witt-ku-witt-kwi-oo" of the screech owl, that sounds like "come with, come with, be soothed"; there was an uneasiness in her that she tried to cover over with singing, prayer, embroidery. She still had not finished the well. She watched the nimble fingers of the others and was at a loss how to complete the three figures at the well. At night she tried to sense whether the floor admitted the dampness from the mountain; she lay down on the stones, her hands beneath her head, saw the night outside the window, listened to the rain, the wind, it will soon be autumn, listened to the hissing of the owls.

> The owl is warm and has the habits of a thief, who knows the day but avoids it, and loves the night. It hates the other birds because it does not like their nature. It knows beforehand when a person is about to die. It senses where sorrow is about to enter, and hastens to the spot like a vulture, but flies away again before the sadness erupts.[2]

She got up again, walked back and forth in her cell, back and forth, always four steps each way, put her footstool before the window and climbed on it to see the stars. The firmament is held together by the stars, Volmar had said. Perhaps Abbot Burkhard knew more about it; did he not stand in the night sometimes and look at the stars? Her father is there, he makes a cradle with his arms and Hildegard climbs in, her legs around his hips, her head on his right shoulder. He carries her across the field; the heaven is high and full of stars.

[1] *De operatione Dei,* 156.
[2] *Naturkunde,* 113.

Look up, see the great bear and the little bear running down, see Cassiopeia dancing. Can you find the seven sisters? Her arms are firmly fixed around her father's neck when she is dizzy from all the stars. The air is tender, her father's steps rock her and she is quiet. And then the star shattering on her forehead.

Abbot Burkhard is very different from her father, shorter, with thin hands that sometimes look bluish and as if he had no arms. It is a shame that she cannot walk with him under the starry sky. She has to be happy when he comes occasionally and discusses something with Jutta, so that Jutta is happier afterward, when he visits us and admires the altar cloth, lifts my head and lets me look into his eyes, great eyes of night, dark brown and not shifting back and forth, eyes that, when he is distributing communion, drop their upper lids like shades. He turns from the altar, the ciborium held in both hands, wrapped in the stole; he comes with deliberate steps toward the grill until she smells the scent of myrrh from his robe, takes the host between thumb and middle finger, takes careful note of the space between the bars, lays the host on her tongue, his sleeve falling back a little, turns and goes with a more deliberate series of steps back to the altar.

Hildegard heard the groaning of the owl that knows the death of a human being in advance; she was frightened, climbed down from her stool and tried to sleep. Then the death knell rang. The owl senses where there is about to be sorrow and hastens there like a vulture, but flies away before the sadness erupts.

Burkhard's corpse lay on the bier before the altar for three days. Candles flickered; two monks were always there keeping vigil; people came and went; the candles burned down; the monks changed shifts, replaced the candle that made the face of the abbot seem restless as she saw it through the bars of the grill. I will never permit an irremovable grill, iron bars from floor to ceiling, braced, narrowed with rosettes, cutting up the altar, the priest, the cross, the chalice, dividing the monks in the choir and the bier into little squares. To change

115

the bluish stiffness of the hands back into life. Alas, for our distance from one another. Dry as a potsherd is my throat, dry as potsherds my eyes.

"To the victors I will give the hidden manna, and a white stone on which is written a new name that no one knows except the one who receives it."[3] On the third day Hildegard saw how the dead man's forehead grew smooth, the outline of his mouth relaxed into a smile, his face was young and pleasant. A sparkle from the stone in his ring touched her and grew in brilliance, just as a star sometimes does.

> The firmament is held together by the stars, so that it cannot break asunder. The fire in the heavenly bodies moves and is moved and to some degree throws forth sparks like leaping and beating pulses. Now and then the stars reveal in themselves many signs showing whether human beings are acting rightly. But they reveal neither the future nor the thoughts of men and women; only what human beings through their own free will have already made evident or brought into being either in word or in work; only that is shown, since the outward atmosphere receives all these things.[4]

To be in Jutta's cloister, with the stars to show what human beings in their free will, in word and in work, have brought into being, to grow old here and to die on this mountain. The edge of the pew cut into Hildegard's forehead, the warmth of the pine touched her cheeks, no superior person, no saint, she smells the wood. "The pine is an image of strength. Spirits hate pine wood and avoid places where it is found. Sorcery and magic are less effective there than elsewhere."[5] To the victors I will give the hidden manna. The owl is silent, the screech owl is silent. Profession is not a decision. Bells ring, Hiltrud looks happy, Jutta, Jona, Mechthild, Margarethe all look happy. Abbot Burkhard. He smiles. The bishop with such important hands. In the distance her mother and father, she

[3] Revelation 2:17.
[4] *Heilkunde*, 66-67.
[5] *Naturkunde*, 71.

is freezing in her fine dress, the sleeves are narrow. The wreath of candles on her head. The opposite of torpor: blessedness, steadfastness, *caeleste desiderium, caritas.* The tree blasted to the root.

> You must be mad if you believe that in a spark in the ashes you can possess the whole of life. I am a pillar, and all the joy of life is in my mind. In no way do I reject the true life, but everything that is harmful I crush.[6]

Put candles in my hair, light them, I will cause the heavens to blaze. Going up to the altar with a flickering headdress, the red tips of the bishop's shoes, the scent of myrrh in Burkhard's robe, his hand on her head when he has removed the wreath. The journey in the boat, the gliding away of the meadows and trees, the swamp, the crane with the three-edged stone, the lynx's blood. The dry river bed, the sapphire, her father's hand, Gimbert lifts her high, Ludger swings her in a circle. One must always begin with a well. Romulus. Romulus, your blood is warm. *In nomine patris et filii et spiritus sancti.* The veil. The crown of thorns. Why are they weeping, her father and Jutta and Hiltrud? I will also give that one a white stone, and written on it a new name that no one knows. In no way do I reject the true life, but everything that is harmful I crush. The owl announced Burkhard's death.

> The screech owl is warm and loves the night and the moonlight more than the day and the sunshine; but it still loves the day more than the owl does. Since it shrinks from the other birds and does not wish to be seen, it prefers the night. It also shows thieving traits and is often like one who knows not what it does. When its chicks come out of the shells, it thinks at first that they are strangers, and kills them. But when it sees that they do not move it is sad and tears at itself because they are of its own blood. It also knows the joyful and sorrowful sides of the human being. With its song, it joins with the joy of happy people; when people are sad, it shows its own

6 *LVM,* 31.

117

sadness by its silence. When it knows that a human being is about to die, it shows this with only a few sounds, and then is silent.[7]

Stars that show what the human being, in free will, in word and deed, has brought about, and

birds that feel in themselves, many times over, every change in the air, and send forth their voices in accord with these changes; their voices represent the power that enables human beings to speak thoughtfully, to consider many things in advance, before they are public deeds. As the birds are lifted into the air by their feathers and hold themselves in the air everywhere, so is the soul held aloft by its thoughts and spreads itself everywhere.[8]

Stars and birds, even the owl, even the screech owl.

[7] *Naturkunde,* 114.
[8] *Naturkunde,* 105.

A fish wishes to go on land,
foam sprays from its mouth,
its body makes a white curve,
its tail fins circle,
dive back into the sea,
fling the body on land
with the power of a bear,
with the force of a lion,
its mouth is ready,
and she puts her hand into it,
her face mirrored twice over
in the goggling eyes,
you must not save me
nor protect me,
I offer myself,
fearlessly full of fear,
a belt made from
your skin on my hips.

XIII

Blackbirds

Coif and bell, prayer and work, sleep strengthens the marrow, prayer and work, the new cloister building is growing, the altar cloth is more and more colorful, the crane stands with lifted foot.

In the first month, the sun begins its upward course. But it shows itself as cold and moist, full of contradictions; it sweats water that has been changed into white snow. The second month, by its nature, tends toward cleansing. The third month arrives with a wild whirlwind. It brings bad weather. Even though there is much that is unhealthy in it, with its manifold winds it sets the seeds of the earth in motion. The fourth month is full of greening life and good odors, even though it can bring terrible thunderstorms. The fifth month is lovely and light and glorious in all the things of the earth. The sixth month, with its heat, is rather dry. To promote good growth it makes its nature mild with every breath of air that ripens the fruit, and yet it sometimes pours out excessive floods of water. The seventh month burns with the full heat of the sun and possesses great power. It ripens the fruits of the earth and dries them. Its weather wavers between drought and floods of rain; it is full of passion. The eighth month comes on in the fullness of power, like a mighty ruler who governs his whole realm in the plenitude of his strength. Therefore it exudes joy. It burns with the singing sun, and because of a certain moisture it brings the dew with it. It can also bring terrible thunderstorms, since the sun is turning towards its decline once more. The ninth month is the time of ripening. No more dreadful storms mar its face. It draws out all the worthless juices from the fruits, and makes them palatable. All this it bears securely through time, as in a sack. The tenth month is like a seated person. It no longer rushes forward in the full power of its greening freshness of life, and it no longer possesses the full warmth of life. Instead, it decorates the foliage of the trees by sweating the cold out of them. The eleventh month comes stooping. It increases the cold and shows none of the joy of summer. It brings the melancholy of winter. Cold breaks forth from it, falls on the earth and draws up the filth. The twelfth month is powerfully cold. The earth grows hard and freezes. Winter covers the land with frozen foam and makes it irksome and arduous. In the first month the sun begins its upward course again.[1]

Prayer and work, waking, sleep strengthens the marrow, work and prayer. Bell and coif. Year after year. Linden and beech. Owl and screech owl, who join their song with the happy mood of some, and by their silence show others, the sorrowing, their sadness; with a few sounds they indicate their knowledge that a human being is about to die.

In this winter the weather was continually changing. Scarcely had it stopped snowing and begun to freeze when warm winds arose, melting the ice and snow; then, when the air had just been delivered from the fall wind, a new cold spell began, clear and hard, quickly changing into mist and wet snow. Bodies did not know how to adjust, and Jutta often grabbed suddenly at her heart.

One day she was called to a sick farm woman. She did not want to respond to the request; just walking through the garden was a strain. But when the abbot ordered her to do it, she went, accompanied by Hiltrud. She returned in time for the midday meal, but ate nothing, did not take her hands from her sleeves, listened to the reading, went into the chapel and did not leave it until after Compline, not taking her hands from her sleeves; she went to her cell.

Hildegard went looking for Hiltrud. What happened? Hiltrud stared bleakly. Speak. But Hiltrud shook her head. Speak. Hildegard shook her by the shoulders. Jutta had gone to the sickbed and stroked the woman's tight-gripped hands: stand up, you are well, you can go back to work. The woman had straightened her bent fingers, wept, laughed, kissed Jutta's hands and stood up. Hildegard said nothing, but laid her arm

[1] *De operatione Dei* I. 4. 98. See *Welt und Mensch,* 153-63.

around Hiltrud. Go on. Jutta had gone out in front or her, silent, looking neither left nor right, only straight ahead, her hands in her sleeves. And then she crossed over the water of the river, not on the footbridge, no, two meters away across the water and with the same stride onto the bank and beyond. You know the rest. Don't talk about it, said Hildegard, and try to sleep; she took Hiltrud's sandals from her feet and covered her with a blanket, snuffed the candle. Jutta lay sleeping, her hands under her back.

Pater noster, ne nos inducas in tentationem, sed libera nos.[2] Do not let Jutta die; do not let her die!

But Jutta was at Matins. Hildegard and Hiltrud did not look closely at her, but they saw her hands in her sleeves. The day passed as usual. Alas, for our distance from one another. The weather had turned, and warm wind rushed around the house. *O vos angeli, qui custoditis populos, vos archangeli, principatus, dominationes, vos cherubim et seraphim, qui custoditis populos!*[3]

How clear Mechthild's voice is, thought Hildegard at the evening meal. The bread is crisp and still warm, and the well water tastes like mead. Jutta sat upright and enclosed the cup with her hands in the sleeves of her habit, as if it were the chalice.

At Compline her lips did not move.

This night also, Hildegard did not sleep. She would have liked to lie down by Jutta, but she did not even look at her. Alas, for our distance from one another. And then, among the calls of the screech owls, she heard a singing, buzzing and jubilation. The whole garden is full of blackbirds. Then she knew for certain, listened a little longer, harking to the buzzing and singing. Then she went to Jutta, smoothed her twisted, knotted fingers and clasped the hands together. *Jubeas eam a*

---

[2] Our Father, lead us not into temptation, but deliver us.

[3] O you angels who guard the peoples, you archangels, principalities, dominations, you cherubim and seraphim, who guard the peoples! *Symphonia* IV. 30. 1–2, 5, 10, 14–15.

sanctis angelis suscipi et ad patriam paradisi perduci. Jubeas eam a sanctis angelis suscipi. Ad patriam paradisi.[4] Human, oh human, set in the place of the fallen creatures of light, companion, partner in the choir. When God looked into the face of the human being, God was very pleased. But then all words failed, and Hildegard wept. She wept until Matins, when the bell rang and she had to give the news and the death knell drove out the song of the blackbirds

For three days the flocks of blackbirds came, morning and evening, and sang. For three days Hildegard saw Jutta's face and hands, through the bars of the candle-illuminated grill, and she had no more words in her soul.

Hildegard was chosen as Jutta's successor. She resisted, begged for time to think, but she knew for certain that she would have to accept the election. Take someone who is stronger than I. I don't know anything about buying and breeding, I can't ring the bell, I can't see behind the sisters' faces, I know nothing, I am nothing. Don't choose me. But she had a portion in land and cup. Human, oh human, set in the place of the fallen creatures of light, companion, partner in the choir. When God looked into the face of the human being, God was very pleased.

Bird, image of strength. "The blackbird is warm and dry and tame, likes to live in pure air and grows from it. One should dry its liver and carry it at all times. It keeps away the devil, who hates it because of its purity."[5] I do not need a blackbird's liver, I need the heart of a heron.

Hiltrud was sick; she did not eat or speak, and refused to get up. You must write it down, that about the farm woman, the walking on water, and about Jutta's hands, the wine and the blackbirds, Hildegard said softly: true or false, natural or miraculous, we poor creatures. Come back to yourself. The

[4] May the holy angels receive her and lead her to her home in paradise.
[5] *Naturkunde*, 115.

water tastes like water again. But Hiltrud did not react. Hildegard sat by her as often as she could, laid cooling cloths on her forehead, caressed her hands, sank down in sorrow. *Jubeas eam a sanctis angelis suscipi et ad patriam paradisi perduci.*[6] And Jutta, do you know her? The woman from Sponheim, do you mean? No, I don't know her, never saw her, only heard her name. Tell me what you know. I can't tell you anything, because I don't know anything. She is supposed to be a good woman. Why do you ask? There she stands, tall and bright. Thirty years.

[6] May the holy angels receive her and lead her to her home in paradise.

Ashes of the Vines

Something—not a human being, not an ape, not a dog—an angular head, no neck, a squarish rump, short legs, covered over and over with dark brown fur up to the ears that emerge from the head. Its eyes are lightless. It jumps up on Hildegard, she smells the musty fur; two hands grasp her neck, the thumbs press her throat, the other fingers are too short to meet around her neck, but they grasp tightly, the pressure on her throat increases. Two rows of teeth gleam, but the eyes remain dead, or is there a flickering in them? Before Hildegard can be sure, the monster jumps down and runs away, gesturing to her to follow.

A tunnel opens before her, covered, the walls hung with dead birds: gaping beaks, feathers that float up and down, birds' hearts; the deformed thing beckons Hildegard farther, pine trees with brown needles, roots reaching upward, outstretched, hung with birds' corpses. The path ends in a room full of habits; there is a musty smell, the habits swing, wind themselves about Hildegard's legs, her body, her throat, there is scratchy wool in her face, a gag in her mouth. The bared teeth of the monster. The lightless eyes.

Hildegard sat up; I should discover an herb against nightmares. She saw before her a bouquet of white leaves and thorns, with fruits like beans that must be laid in the fire, roasted and ground; then the image dissolved. Probably we are not eating properly. You recommended two cooked dishes, St. Benedict; whoever cannot eat one, can be adequately nourished from the other. But if fruit and fresh vegetables are available, one may offer a third dish. A full pound of bread is sufficient for one day. And wine? We should not drink to repletion, but should be abstemious. Permit that which brings joy. We are all weak.

> Food should be distributed for refreshment in the right measure, so that among the faithful followers there should be no lack of joy in the soul. If human beings nourish their flesh in moderation, their behavior is also happy and sociable. But when they surrender themselves to an excess of feasting and carousing, they plant within themselves the seeds of every shameful fault. And anyone who, on the other hand, damages his or her body by unreasonable asceticism goes about everywhere with an angry manner. From dry rocks spring nothing but thorns and useless things.[7]

We must pay more attention to combinations, not forget variety, once a month have something special that refreshes the gums and warms the stomach. Could Wineldis do it better than Altriede? It is wrong to despise God's earth. No martyrdom. St. Benedict, I am a bad monastic. It was good that the bell called for Matins.

I lie down and sleep; I wake again, for the Lord sustains me. I am not afraid of the thousands of people who have set themselves against me all around. Rise up, O Lord! Deliver me, O my God! For you strike all my enemies on the cheek;

[7] *Heilkunde* 280, 279.

you break the teeth of the wicked. But was there not, after all, a flickering in the dead eyes of the monster? For you strike all my enemies on the cheek; you break the teeth of the wicked.[8] Dead birds, slaughtered trees. I wake again, for the Lord sustains me. Partner in the choir. Set in the place of the fallen angels. When God looked upon the human countenance, God was exceedingly pleased.[9]

After Prime, Hildegard went out of the cloister and scattered snow left and right. There was not much snow; single flakes glittered bluish in the morning moonlight. She caught a few flakes and let them melt in her hand, took up a handful of snow and washed her face, gathered another handful and ate it. How dry my throat is. To lie in the snow, press down with her head, close her spread legs, make wings with her arms. Snow angels. Odilia called them eagles. But when you get up you destroy the image; even if the sisters stood left and right to help, its purity was lost. To make an angel print now, here in the morning moonlight that gives the snow a bluish gleam. The morning star is reddening, but the evening star will profit by it. She swept the path to the gate and was content. Sick people were already waiting.

So many tooth problems, petrifactions, decay, pus and blood, pain. That is because of the winter, thought Hildegard, they sleep too long with decaying food in their mouths, they get no fruit or vegetables.

> Those who wish to have sound, strong teeth should, early in the morning when they get out of bed, take pure, cold water in the mouth and hold it there a long while, so that the sticky film that has gathered on the teeth may be softened. The teeth should be cleaned with the same water that was held in the mouth; this should be done frequently, in order that the film may not accumulate around the teeth. Thus they will remain sound. If the flesh around the teeth rots, or if the teeth are

8 Psalm 3:5-7.
9 *De operatione Dei* I. 4. 100.

> unsound, one should mix wine with warm grapevine ashes, and with this wine the teeth and gums should be cleansed. This must be done frequently, and then the flesh will be healed and the teeth will be made firm. But even if the teeth are sound, such a cleansing will do them good and make them beautiful.[10]

Hildegard cleansed, rinsed, laid packing made from the bones of salmon and the juice of nightshade around the teeth, here and there slit the gums with a thorn so that the pus could run out, gave advice, stroked a cheek or a shoulder. And then, as she was cleaning it, one of the old farmer's teeth broke off. She was shocked at her own clumsiness and at the yellow, corroded fragment in her hand. She had pulled teeth with a thread or a pair of pincers, but the root of a tooth? If I do not take it out it will get infected and cause unspeakable pain.

She laid a sedative wrapping of herbs around the man's jaw, then sat down quickly, told the farmer to place his head in her lap and to grip the legs of the chair with his hands; she cut the jaw open right and left, front and back with short, rapid strokes; now she could grasp the root with the pincers and loosen it. Tears ran from the man's eyes and sweat from his brow, his body was twisted. Hildegard sang while she loosened the root and the old man relaxed; now she could pull out the root. So, it hurt, but only for a short time instead of for a long time. She took a cloth and wiped the tears from the poor man's eyes, the sweat from his face and from her own forehead. Dear God, she thought, I was lucky, but don't let me become a dentist! She left the rest of the treatment to Clementia. I will start Terce a little early.

She laid her thumb and middle finger on the bridge of her nose. The morning star is reddening, and the evening star will profit by it. She saw the bluish glitter of the snow in the morning moonlight. Thought of the monster. You strike all my enemies on the cheek.

---

[10] *Heilkunde*, 252. See *Medicine*, 15–16.

A Tuft of Hair

Then Jacob took one of the stones from the place and laid it under his head, and he lay down in that place. And he dreamed that there was a ladder set up on the earth, the top of it reaching to heaven; and the angels of God were ascending and descending on it.[11]

"Gain-a, gain-a, er-high?" called Gimbert, and Hildegard called "er-high, er-high," hoping that the wind would carry it away, but it did not, and Gimbert gripped both ropes and let her fly, so that the two trees shook gently and groaned. "Nough-e, nough-e," cried Hildegard, just before swinging over the top, something she longed for and feared at the same time. "Nough-e, nough-e!" Gimbert caught the swing: "Eth thear ash ouy gain-a." Her back strained a little, her feet scuffed on the ground, the dancing field, the tumbling pine trees again stood fixed and straight. Hildegard jumped from the swing: "at-tha si ifel, ksanth, ksanth," and kissed Gimbert's chest.

The arrangement of the ladder, oh St. Benedict, two shafts, twelve steps. Faults in thought, of the tongue, the hands, the feet, the will, the reports of the angels. I have nothing to do with things that are too wonderful and high. But snow can have a bluish gleam in the morning moonlight.

Hildegard removed her fingers from the bridge of her nose and was startled when she saw Richardis and Volmar. I have finished the papers for the field, the vineyard, the forest section, and also for the movable goods, said Volmar softly. You only need to sign them. Yes, yes. The new sisters had brought good dowries with them. Donata, Criseldis, Clementia, Abilgard. But there are still some letters. Twelve steps, two shafts, er-high, er-high. Hildegard tried to shake the stiffness from her neck. So, write. They want to know why you only admit

[11] Genesis 28:11-12.

women from respected and noble families. Hildegard groped for words, swallowed them, tried again. The bluish light, the dry throat, the cramping in the toes. The angels' reporting, faults of the will.

> The regulation (of class differences) is God's business. God takes care that the lower class should not elevate itself above the upper, as Satan and the first human beings did, since they desired to fly higher than their station. Who would place all their livestock in a single stable—oxen, donkeys, sheep, goats—and would they not separate themselves? Therefore one should preserve the differences here in order that those who come from different levels among the people may not split apart in proud arrogance because they are shamed by their class differences, as they might do if they were grouped together in a single flock. But especially it is so that class honor may not be damaged when they tear one another apart in hatred—when the higher class attacks the lower and the lower places itself above the higher. For it is good that human beings not seek to take control over a mountain that they cannot move from its place, but rather that they remain in the valley and gradually learn what they can do. [12]

Volmar wrote. It was impossible to see what he was thinking. Richardis nodded agreement. Yes, thought Hildegard, it is good that human beings should not seek to take control of a mountain that they cannot move from its place. If anyone strikes you on the right cheek, turn the other also, and if anyone wants to sue you and take your coat, give your cloak as well; and if anyone forces you to go one mile, go also the second mile. [13] St. Benedict. Gain-a, gain-a, er-high. The angels go up and down. A double movement. We should invent a secret language, discover the original language. *No eth ainmount oot soombl eth denlin.* She let the words dissolve on her tongue; she said nothing. I am always turning aside, but I

[12] *Briefe,* 203.
[13] Matthew 5:39-40.

do not occupy myself with things too great and too marvelous for me.[14]

A farmer is there calling for help, his wife has been in labor for three days already. It had been agreed with Abbot Kuno that the women should not leave the house. Herb garden, ointment kitchen, bath house, treatment of the sick, yes, but no leaving the cloister. What business is it of his, thought Hildegard, this is my affair. She called Clementia and followed the farmer. Mist wafting; the path is slippery. I only know Kuno's face with bars across it, don't know his eyes, his gesture of blessing is narrow, his hand with the host is wooden, but it is not right, is there not enough disturbance before the house, enough groaning and weeping? The rule is the rule, and the ways are dangerous. He is a good businessman, a clever builder, his face is rosy. How was that again? *No eth ainmount oot soombl eth denlin.* Must I not follow where I am called? What will you do, then, asked Clementia, cut open her body and pull out the child?

In the hut things looked bad. The pillows were bitten through, there were feathers and bunches of hair in the air, the thick body was writhing and bucking, there were cries like those at a slaughtering. Two farm women, wet with sweat, held the laboring woman under the arms. Lay her down. The mouth of the womb was closed, the muscles like stone, but she could hear the heartbeat. Tea to promote contractions. Breathe with me. Soft, circular motions on body and thighs, shoulders and neck. Breathe with me. Groaning, shrieks, mouth of the womb closed. Eyes staring from their sockets, the body wet. Breathe with me. Soft, circular motions. The contractions are faster, stronger, the mouth of the womb still closed. Then Hildegard lays a bunch of hair on the woman's belly. Breathe with me. She places her hand in the vagina, and Clementia pushes Hildegard's hand aside, grasps the little head, and pulls the child out. Blood, mucus, filth. The child

---

[14] Psalm 131:1.

132

is blue, but it cries. The women take care of the little bundle and of the mother. Hildegard sits drooping. The angels' reporting. My heart is not lifted up, my eyes are not raised too high; I do not occupy myself with things that are too great and too marvelous for me.[15]

Compline was long past when the women returned to the cloister. They went silently to their cells. Hildegard took the bunch of hair from her pocket, shook her head, laid it aside, knelt on her bed and laid her head on her arms. What a beastly squalling, mucus and blood. And the child? Then she fell asleep. She goes through the dead garden to the well, places her hand on the water, mirrors her face, sees nothing. She walks by a trellis of winter roses, but none of the buds opens. The gate opens and a wave of white moisture rolls toward her, twists before her nose, floods into her lungs, crushes her breath. Wetness soaks upward on her skirt, her foot does not know where it is stepping. That is the river; she will not walk on water, she is not Jutta. She pushes the wisps of fog from her eyes.

A lynx appears, a whole crowd of them; they each bear a jacinth on a lifted paw. She knows that no one should drink jacinth water, "or they will lose their life, since the power of this medium is so strong that it would devour the heart, split and crush the head."[16] The jacinth does not shine in the dampness. The lynxes let the stones fall on their other paw and run away; she falls and lies there, her mouth full of ancient leaves, she crawls to the river, hangs her face over the water to wash out the leaves, the water begins to sparkle and the leaves in her mouth bloom into gold, catch her eye, a great brightness gathers, shrinks to dots, eyes, and the eyes rest on four wings, and the four wings belong to a figure with extended arms; the eyes shine.

No, I will mend torn skin, assuage the pains of childbirth, stanch blood. Hildegard bowed her head, her shoulders

---

[15] Ibid.
[16] *Steine,* 68.

straight, and tried to steady her knees. Her back beaten with switches. Failings in thought, of the tongue, the hands and feet and the will. I have nothing to do with things that are too wonderful and high for me. Attraction toward love. Reporting of the angels. Longing for light, and the inability to bear it. I am cowardly. A fragile person, shy, simple, unlearned. She walked back and forth in the cell, shook her limbs. "You have scarcely begun to follow the way of God when the buzzing of flies and mosquitoes frightens you back."[17] Jacob's beautiful dream. We would be like the birds that stare at their reflection in the water, and since they pay no more attention to anything else, they die very quickly. She feels the cold, she cannot shake the stiffness out of her. With wooden steps she follows the bell to Matins.

[17] *Scivias* III. 9. 1. See *HB* 452.

The Buzzing of Flies and Mosquitoes

My soul is cast down within me; therefore I remember you from the land of Jordan and of Hermon, from Mount Mizar. Deep calls to deep at the thunder of your cataracts; all your waves and your billows have gone over me.[18]

How have the sisters slept? Mechthild's voice is as strong and bright as ever; one cannot pick out Jona's; Criseldis articulates too sharply, and Ursula is singing off key again; how pale Richardis is; Bertha must have fever, she cannot swallow; Hiltrud's cadences are gentle.

What kind of day will it be? Will they sing at their weaving and spinning, cooking and cleaning, break bread with contentment, look at each other in a friendly way? Why are you

[18] Psalm 42:6-7.

cast down, O my soul, and why are you disquieted within me?[19] Criseldis is annoyed at the brothers' feeble ringing; Wineldis complains about wet firewood; Clementia's ointment was a failure; Alfriede scalded her hand. And then, before the siesta began, Ursula stood up. She wanted to speak for all the sisters: we get up too early, we should at least wait for sunrise; breakfast should be laid after the morning services, something hot, strengthening; there should not be specialization for garden, bakery, scriptorium and so on; and in the evening there should be a group discussion of problems. It is excessive to get up at two in the morning, to be nine hours without food, it is deadly to stand at the gate or the oven year after year and to discuss every want in private. Hildegard listened. Failings in thought and of the tongue, hands and feet and the will, twelve steps, two shafts. The angels' reporting. We must keep the rule, she says quietly.

> We need not live continually in silence. What is appropriate, and the necessary questions that arise, should be discussed among us, so that no antipathy shall arise through improper silence.[20]

Anyone who wishes to speak should come to me. And as far as eating and drinking are concerned, "for a person in good health it is right and helpful for a good digestion not to eat breakfast, but instead to delay it until shortly before midday."[21] However, if anyone is ill, she should tell me.

> When someone is suffering from a great sorrow, that person should eat heartily of those foods that agree with him or her, in order to be revived by food, since sorrow has weighed the person down so much. But anyone who is very boisterous should eat moderately, since through the expansion of the blood vessels the blood is released and then, if one eats too

---

[19] Psalm 42:5.
[20] *Heilkunde,* 277.
[21] Ibid., 193. See *Medicine,* 44.

much, the juices contained in the blood may get out of control, resulting in stormy and feverish conditions. [22]

Still more softly she said:

> You should cultivate your own plot of earth within yourself, in order that it may not dry out and become unfruitful. But for this you must assemble yourself with all the strength of your heart, and concentrate on one thing, in order that you may not make your heart accustomed to the changeableness of restless moods. Fundamentally, you are like the good earth that is frequently saturated by an appropriate measure of moisture in order that it may bring forth lovely and desirable plants. [23]

She spoke the closing prayer and left the sisters.

She went and bandaged Alfriede's hand, went and painted Bertha's throat, went to Ursula, who had taken off her veil and coif and gathered together her prayerbook, crucifix, and rosary. If the unbeliever wishes to separate, let it be so! In this way, one unruly sheep will not infect the whole flock, so said St. Benedict. I know everything you will say against me now, said Ursula; spare your words. I have thought it all over long and thoroughly. Release me from my vows and let me go. Hildegard thought of St. Benedict and was silent. She sat down on Ursula's bed and stared at her sandals. When she finally looked up, Ursula had gone. I am not in command of the blessing, she thought; Mechthild will settle everything. So one unruly sheep will not infect the whole flock. She went into her cell and lay down. The sparkling river, the leaves in her mouth. The angels' reporting. Failings in thought, of the tongue, the hands and feet.

Nails are driven into her toes, tenfold, the tendons are fastened into her heels with screws, lead is poured into the veins of her legs, into her intestines, her stomach, her kid-

[22] *Heilkunde,* 194.
[23] Ibid., 280.

neys, boiling lead, staples are driven into her larynx, her teeth are being riveted with iron pegs, one tooth at a time, a clamp is being screwed into her tongue, the tears are freezing in her eyes.

The worship services went on, the work was done, meals were eaten. She will die, they all thought, looking at one another with strange eyes. Clementia wrapped Hildegard in warm cloths, but the cloths stiffened; Hiltrud tried to pour hot wine into her, but the wine ran out the corners of her mouth. Not a sound. Not a breath. The sisters wept. My soul is cast down within me; therefore I remember you from the land of Jordan and of Hermon, from Mount Mizar. Deep calls to deep at the thunder of your cataracts; all your waves and your billows have gone over me.[24] Richardis held Hildegard's head in her two hands till Jona relieved her, till Hiltrud relieved Jona, till Richardis pushed Hiltrud aside. We must have patience, said Mechthild. The abbot came. The abbot called for help from Mainz, they turned Hildegard from her back to her side. A little water flowed from her. Let her rest, begged Richardis. The sisters wept; Volmar sat deeply bowed in his seat. The worship services went on, the work was done, meals were eaten. A death house.

After forty days Hildegard awoke, drew up her knees, asked for a glass of water from the well, drank it in tiny sips. Then she slept for three days and three nights, breathing deeply. The clamp loosened itself from her tongue, the pegs, rivets, staples, screws and nails dissolved, warmth returned to her body. Failings in thought, of the hands and feet, of the will. Angels ascend and descend the ladder. Double movement. Reporting. The sparkling river, the leaves from her mouth a golden blooming. Your waves and floods broke over me. The light says: the law creates life, the darkness divisions. The human being who desires to possess life must be free of divisions. Know the ways.

[24] Psalm 42:6-7.

J acob's
beautiful dream,
the morning star
is reddening.
I
have nothing to do
with things that
are too wonderful
for me,
my heart
is not proud.
If your shirt
is stolen,
leave your cloak
as well.
Blood, mucus, pus,
pincers and screws.
An angel
of snow,
er-high, er-high.
The sparkling water.
Partner in the choir,
in place of the light.

XIV

The Iron-Colored Mountain

I looked and saw something like a great, iron-colored mountain. Enthroned upon it was such a glorious figure of light that its magnificence blinded my eyes. From both sides of this ruler extended an opaque shadow, like wings wonderfully broad and long. Before him, at the foot of the mountain, there stood a being covered all over with eyes—so much so that I could not even make out the human features beneath the eyes. In front of this being there stood another, like a young child, wearing a dull-colored gown and white shoes. Over its head there flowed, from the one seated on the mountain, such a fullness of glory that I could not even look on the face of this little girl. There also went forth from the one seated on the mountain many living and glowing sparks that flew very sweetly around the figures. The mountain itself contained a great many tiny windows in which appeared human heads, some of subdued colors and some white.[1]

Hildegard spoke slowly, breathing regularly to curb her trembling. Fragile human being, dust from dust, ashes from ashes. For the lukewarm and the dull, who timidly buried the mystery, fruitlessly, in a hidden field. Her voice was soft, gripping Volmar's big ear. She rested her feet on the stool, the tablet on her lap, inscribing words in the wax: mountain, light, wing, shadow, living sparks, glowing. To the timid fearless ones. Dust from dust. "In the shadow of your wings I will take refuge. Do not cut me off from the land of the living."[2] The wax was pliant. If one were to ignite it, it would give forth the scent of Arabia.

Volmar, as Hildegard could hear, often dared to breathe only enough to keep life in his body, and he had learned to get by with little breath during these hours; later, in the garden, he would make up for it. Do not cut me off from the land of the living.

---

[1] *Scivias* I. See *HB* 67.
[2] Ibid., III; see *HB* 310; Psalm 57:1; Isaiah 53:8.

A path between bushes twined with honeysuckle, stones under her soles, a magpie. *Vere dignum et justum est, aequum et salutare,*[3] the rhythm of the habits. The green of the statues fluoresces. Five untamable wild onrushes of temporal systems of authority. The world is in such a state that, while existing in the certain possession of its powers, it yet inclines toward its own fall. Five wild beasts: the fiery dog, the yellow lion, the pale horse, the black pig, the grey wolf. In the era of the pig, "the leaders will blacken themselves with misery. They will put aside the divine law, and diverge from the commandments of God."[4] Do you know anything about sorrow?

> If God's grace does not come swiftly to rescue the soul, this depression can develop into a spiritual paralysis and cause disdain, hardening and obstinacy in the human person. It fetters the soul's forces. When such a person encounters resistance, he or she is easily aroused to hatred and other deadly passions that murder the soul and leave it in ruins and decay.[5]

Do not cut me off from the land of the living. And after the age of the grey wolf?

> At this end, through a sudden and unexpected shaking, the elements will be loosed from their moorings; all creation will be set in motion, fire will break forth, air will dissolve, water will overflow, earth will collapse, lightning strike, thunder roar, mountains split, forests fall, and everything that is in the air or in the water or on the earth will expire. For fire will penetrate the whole air and water will flood the whole earth. And so all will be cleansed, so that everything hateful in this world will disappear as if it had never existed, just as salt dissolves when it is cast into water.[6]

And then? Then will come the resurrection of the body to judgment.

[3] It is truly right and just, meet and good for [our] salvation.
[4] *Scivias* III. 11. 5. See *HB* 494–95.
[5] *Scivias* I. 4. 22. See *HB* 122.
[6] Gronau, 146.

Often, after dictating, Hildegard suffered from one of her states of exhaustion. The vessel of her body felt as if it were being baked in a potter's oven. She laid the tablet aside, let her head and arms fall, closed her eyes, was still for a few seconds, collected herself. She pushed herself up from her chair, went to Volmar and laid her hands on his shoulders, her forehead against his forehead. Then the tips of their noses may have touched, and when she opened her eyes she saw herself reflected in Volmar's eyes.

I am quite awake, she then said softly and calmly; it is true that these are not the eyes of the body nor the ears of the outer self, but rather the eyes and ears within, if anyone knows what that means.[7] Volmar nodded, suggested another word, revised a sentence, found the Latin word, wall of light, wall of stone, threefold wall, three-faced column, shining wall, closed wall that becomes a pierced grill. The devil's booth, shadows of light green folds. He rewrote it all when Hildegard went away to care for the sick, greet a pilgrim, sniff a new ointment, taste the salad for the evening meal, practice a song with the others. Was Volmar also a vessel baked in the potter's oven? No curse must grow in the pit of his stomach, she thought. But it must be written. Do not cut us off from the land of the living. The hours of revision became easier. Volmar read what he had written, Hildegard revised it, Richardis corrected her version and, together with Volmar, composed the final version under Hildegard's direction. A tedious task; often they only produced four or five lines, sometimes a page. Whatever was not finished lay ready to be taken up again, tomorrow or the next day. Ten long years.

"The king crossed the Wadi Kidron, and all the people moved on toward the wilderness."[8]

Dust from dust, ash from ashes. "I, a human being, who does not glow as does the strong lion."[9] Place forehead to fore-

[7] See *Scivias,* "Declaration" (*HB* 60).
[8] 2 Samuel 15:23.
[9] *Scivias* II. 1; see *HB* 149.

head so that the tips of the noses touch. I will draw myself up by these ears when I do not know how to go on. When there were still ten minutes left before Vespers they probably went a few steps together through the garden, silent, breathing deeply, leaning on the rim of the well, until Hildegard drew her hand through the water so that the two faces melted into one another. But they did not laugh. They heard the bell, the plectrum, the shuddering flanks. The king crossed the Wadi Kidron, and all the people moved on toward the wilderness. "If a human being cannot bear my yoke, I will take that person away before the soul begins to wilt and dry up."[10] Look at the evening sky, at the tips of the linden trees. I saw a glorious figure of light on an iron-colored mountain. Then Volmar looked at her from the side and nodded, and it was as if his ear was shining.

[10] *Scivias* I. 3. 24; see *HB* 102–03.

The Cat

The age of the pig and the sorrow that cripples, brings forth hate and destroys the soul, the deviation from the commandments. When I am confined, give me open space. A living treasure is given to you, your reason, and you are commanded "to invest your reason in good works at interest."[11] The person with two voices, thought Hildegard: accomplish good things. Do what desire brings forth in you, the human being, the creature that does not wish to be what it really is. The pencil in her hand lay on the tablet, the wax grew warm and soft. And yet it is a creature of longing, from its very origins. Creature of longing: that is a good expression. Let me out of my confinement into broad spaces. To move on toward the wilderness. She sighed. Write, she said:

[11] Cf. *Scivias* III. 10. 31; *HB* 488–89.

The human being has in itself three paths along which its life moves: the soul, the body, and the senses. The soul gives life to the body and also brings the breath of life to the senses. The body draws the soul to itself and opens the senses. The senses, finally, touch the soul and transmit impulses to the body. Just as fire pours light into the darkness, so the soul gives life to the body. It has two principal powers, like two arms: intellect and will. It is not as if the soul had need of arms in order to move, but it reveals itself in these powers as the sun does by its brilliance. Intellect is that power of the soul to which it belongs particularly to recognize whether a person's actions have anything in them that is good or evil. Like a master, it sees into all things as if it were sifting them, as one cleanses the wheat from the chaff. It seeks to learn whether something is useful or harmful, deserving of love or hate, leading to life or to death. Without it, the other powers of the soul are dull and without discernment, as food without salt is tasteless. The will has great power within the soul; it is the right arm, with which it controls the blood vessels and the marrow and moves the whole body. Like a fire, it bakes every work with its heat, and when it is firm, it pounds it as well. Like yeast, it pours its inner power into the work and crushes it in the mortar of its energy. Then it lets its work ferment through contemplation and finally brings it to perfection through the full action of its ardor.

See, oh human, what you are in your soul! You succeed in throwing away heedlessly your precious gift, the power of reason, and you desire to place yourself on a level with the beasts.[12]

Hildegard was glad when the bell rang for Sext. Did not Volmar and Richardis also lay their pens down with relief? To grind something in the mortar of its energy. Your guardian never sleeps. The shad at your right hand. The sun shall not strike you by day, nor the moon by night. Mechthild's voice is pure and clear; Hiltrud's joins it on a darker note. Clementia probably moves only her lips again. Hildegard

[12] *Scivias* I. 4. 18-19, 21, 26; *HB* 120-24.

wished for a moment that she could embrace her sister, but then she took her hands from her sleeves and folded her fingers together: a commitment willingly undertaken, renunciation of freedom, surrender of the body, ready to suffer and to work. The sun shall not strike you by day, nor the moon by night.

The soup did them good; how clever to stew the meat in little balls, to garnish the beans with parsley; the warm bread did them good, and the cool wine-flavored water; Donata's grey face grew livelier, but Altriede was not a good reader: David danced wearily before the ark, and Michal need not have had so much contempt, and no one took any pleasure in cakes of bread and cakes of raisins.[13] The sisters were overcome with sleepiness. They should take some rest, thought Hildegard.

She herself went into the garden, greedy for air. Roses with strong stems, not yet blooming, their thorns sharp, ideal for opening boils. She pulled off a wilted leaf, rubbed it, smelled its mortality. She picked up a feather: I will wash it and dry it in the sun, it may be good for writing. She dug a hole in the earth and pushed the corpse of a snail into it. She sat down at the well, washed the feather, thought for a moment of Robert. Rain must purify the water. Then she saw the cat, ready to spring, and in the linden tree the dove preening itself. She clapped her hands to startle the dove into flight, but the cat was quicker. It closed its paws around the dove's feet, struck its teeth into the throat, stifled the cry, made the feathers dance, tore out the guts. The dove's head fell at Hildegard's feet as the cat darted away. The drops of blood, the scratched feet of the dove, the head with the neck feathers sticking out, the eyes.

Why did she clap her hands too late? Why did she not drive away the cat with her black habit, why did she not shake the tree at the right moment, why did she not shout a word of warning? Shadows of light-green folds, the devil's booth. She buries the dove's head with its open eyes, shakes the feet from

[13] 2 Samuel 6:16, 19.

145

the twig; the leaves rustle. Wall of light, the devil's booth. The cat will lick its lips and paws. She goes into the scriptorium and sits down in her chair. If I let my shoulders hang, the arrow is not so sharp. She hears the word "idleness," hazy, approaching. In idleness one has no share in the wonderful works of blessedness. She repeats the sentence. To sleep, not to take part any more, it is such an effort to take part. Black cats dance and leap around her, one jumps on her shoulders and puts a bread ring on her head, fixes it fast with its claws, she feels the pulsing blood of the cat, the barbs, the heavy body on her shoulders, the hissing of the others as they dance. One jumps into the bread ring on her head and lifts its forefeet. Thus you are horned.

You fell asleep, Richardis says softly. You must have been dreaming. Drink a sip of water. Eyebrows, mirror of the moon's path, the blow of the wind's wings with which they lift and hold themselves, like a bird that one moment flutters up on its pinions and the next moment rests, floating. Thank you. I must write to Bernard of Clairvaux, I cannot delay any longer, write. But when she was finished, she said: you can put that aside, I must formulate it differently, more precisely. Was she then really more wretched in her existence, as a woman, than she would be otherwise? Had she truly never lived in security from her childhood onward? She had had her father, Gimbert, Romulus, and Ludger. Was she honorable in writing that she had never been secure for a single hour? And what did it really mean: "I will be so easily crushed by the falling beams in the winepress of my nature, growing from the root that, through the devil's influence, arose in Adam, so that he was cast out into the world where there was no homeland?"[14]

Did she see Bernard as someone who was not afraid, but bold? Hildegard sought for other formulations, compared a

[14] Letter to Bernard of Clairvaux (1147); see Fox, ed., *Book of Divine Works,* 271–73.

short letter to a longer one, threw both away, began again. And she was happy when Volmar came, found the first version to be the best and rewrote it in a fair hand. You must write just as it is, he said, and read the whole thing once more, gave it to her for her signature and sealed it. I have also let Abbot Kuno know about the vision, he said then, I did it without your consent, since you would have asked for a delay. The abbot wants to get into contact with the people at Mainz.

Hildegard said nothing. Bernard of Clairvaux was important to her. How long does it take for a letter to get there, will it get lost, will it be mislaid, not read, answered? Writing letters, not seeing in the eyes and corners of the mouth what someone thinks. Wall of light, tower and columns. The sapphire-blue figure that sparkles through and through, in the soft red of a flowing and blazing flame. Sapphire-blue figure. I am the life. I am the fullness of life: not struck from stones, not blooming from twigs, not rooted in the protective power of the man. Instead, everything has its roots in me. Reason is the root; the sounding word blooms from it. I ignite above the beauty of the fields, I shine in the waters and burn in the sun, moon and stars. And the devil's booths? The throat feathers stiffen on the severed head of the dove, the black cat gives me horns.

Invest your reason in good works at interest, draw insight through your understanding, to know whether something is good or evil. I am the fullness of life. Grind the work in the mortar of energy. Do not place yourself on the level of the beasts. Sapphire-blue figure, sparkling in the red of the flowing flame. What does Michal's despising mean? I will play and dance before the Lord. Your guardian never sleeps. The sun shall not strike you by day, nor the moon by night. I am the fullness of life. Will Bernard of Clairvaux answer me? Volmar nodded. The bell has rung for None, he says.

Rupert

Rupert, the son of a pagan father who fell in battle against the Christians, was brought up by his mother Bertha, daughter of a noble Christian family, and the priest Wigbert. He was a pilgrim of Rome who died at age twenty, a friend of God, one of those who left the shipwreck of the world after having taken to himself the excluded and despised and the lost sheep. He was not swallowed by the dance in the ancient cave, but entered into the wall of living stones.[15] *O felix apparitio. O beatissime Ruperte!*[16] Leaping sparks. Threads of light. There is Rupertsberg. With twenty nuns from noble families and rich parents, I will take up my abode in this place. We will find no dwelling there, except for that of an old man, his wife, and children. Great resistance. The burden of work. Affliction. We lack the necessities of life. People shake their heads: what good does it do for noble and rich nuns to leave a place where they lacked for nothing and go to such a miserable place? Threads of light, leaping sparks. *O felix apparitio, beatissime Ruperte!*

Uncertainty. Nails are driven into her toes, screws twist the sinews of her heels, her teeth are hammered with iron pegs, the tears freeze in her eyes. To snatch her out of oblivion. Richardis's cool hands. Eyebrows like the beating of the wings of the morning wind. Mirror of the moon's path by night. Let my face rest in these hands. You cannot turn a boulder around. Threads of light. A gem. A vessel. To leave a world bound for shipwreck and be a citizen of heaven. We are working hard for our own banishment. Living stones in the wall. *Felix apparitio.*

A church with three aisles and two towers. A bell, sometimes I will take turns with Criseldis, the bell will sing across

---

[15] "O Jerusalem," sequence for St. Rupert, *Symphonia* IV. 49. 4b.
[16] O happy apparition (*Symphonia* IV. 46. 1); O most blessed Rupert (*Symphonia* IV. 47. 1).

the fields. A cloister. Do not rouse me, Irmentraut of Stadland, when the ivy blooms. The cells have windows without bars. Anyone who does not wish to stay must go. The wall has a gate. We must start with the well; a water-finder will come, Robert perhaps. Water, healing power. We will bring it from the source into our house, into every cell, cells in which one can walk back and forth and lift the arms high. Workshops, kitchens, stables, a guest house, a place for the sick. *Beatissime Ruperte.*

To take to oneself the lost sheep, the excluded, the despised, not to be swallowed by the dance in the ancient cave. An herb garden, the dill is knee-high. Iris illyrica, ferns, I take the seeds on my tongue. A date palm. A linden. Chestnut seedlings for the crosier. *O felix apparitio.* A song about the friend of God. Whom are they bringing there, trembling, choking on the thick tongue that the mouth can no longer contain? Now he lays out the graves under the beeches, clears the field. I will cultivate the vineyard myself. Threads of light. Leaping sparks. *O beatissime Ruperte.*

Help me, Robert, bring me the clay, bring me the stones, I stroke the backs of the oxen. Look how malleable the clay is and how it spreads, and see the stones, shot through with sun, how they arrange themselves, order themselves, above and below, the wind makes them grow together, the clay and the stones, the stars burn them fast. I will not turn aside from the fragile earth, but will contend valiantly against it. Smell, touch, taste and hear how wonderful life is, how glorious it is to live. We fight for our rights. Anyone who does not wish to remain must go. Volmar I will take with me, and Richardis and Hiltrud and Jona. I will not turn aside from the fragile earth. Sparks of light are everywhere in this shipwrecked world. *Beatissime Ruperte.*

A Bearing Wind

Since writing to Bernard of Clairvaux, Hildegard was calmer. She learned to fall asleep quickly in the evening, and she also learned to take a short nap at midday, after which she arose refreshed and went into the garden to pull weeds, cut off the withered blooms, pick a basket of beans, or went into the ointment kitchen to stir a paste or pulverize a root. In idleness one has no share in the works. A regular and even alternation of relaxation and activity, mental and physical work gave her the strength she needed each day to say what she had seen.

Write just:

> Humanity stands in the middle of the world edifice, for it is more important than all the other creatures which remain dependent on the world. Although small in stature, humanity is mighty in the powers of the soul. Its head directed upward, its feet on firm ground, it is able to set in motion both the things above and the things below. What it effects with the works of its right and left hand penetrates the universe, since in the power of its inner humanityn it has the potential to accomplish such things.[17]

It is clad in the armor of creation, in order that its sight may behold the whole world, understand it by hearing and distinguish it by smell, be nourished by it in taste and control it by touch. Hildegard saw Volmar's questioning glance. Yes, yes, that is quite correct: what it brings about with a single work penetrates the universe. It is both creature and creator. That is the demand of the creator God, that it, the human being, should work in the world in virtue of its reason, this human being, the black, filthy clay, the weak, vulnerable, suffering clay that possesses the Living One within its heart. Think of the sapphire-blue figure: vulnerability of existence and yet mirror of all the wondrous works of God, that is the

---

[17] *De operatione Dei* I. 2. 15.

human being, in the heart of the Living One, black clay, surrounded by precious stones and pearls. Hildegard laid her hand over her eyes, was silent, saw storms rushing upon the human being and bending it to earth. Just write, she said softly:

> I, a pilgrim! Where am I? In the shadow of death. By what path am I journeying? The path of error. What consolation have I? The consolation of those who are pilgrims. I should have had a tabernacle bedecked with five square gems, more brilliant than the sun and the stars, for this sun and these stars that set would not have shone in it, but rather the glory of the angels. A topaz would have been its foundation, and its walls of nothing but precious stones, its stairs made of crystal, its courtyards paved with gold. For I have been called to be the companion of the angels, since I am the living breath sent by God into the dry clay. Therefore I should have known God and felt God. But alas! When my tabernacle saw that with its eyes it could behold the whole world, it turned its attention to the north. Alas! Alas! There I was made captive, robbed of my sight and the joy of knowledge. My gown is torn. I have been driven from my inheritance. I was abducted far away, to a place without any beauty or honor. I am delivered to the most shameful servitude.[18]

The bell rang for Vespers. The bell, our scourge. Hildegard withdrew her hand from her eyes. Volmar drew his hood over his head and disappeared with a short, loving wave of the hand in farewell for this day. His lips are bluish, thought Hildegard. I dictate too fast, I must pause more often for him. Farewell for this day. I, a pilgrim, called to be the companion of the angels. Far from home. But I will not turn aside from the fragile earth; I will fight valiantly against it. And she raised her voice: he will drink from the stream by the path, therefore he will lift up his head.[19] And the sisters all joined in.

One day, the gentlemen with sharp ears and eyes came. Abbot Kuno hosted them regally with perch and venison, fruit

---

[18] *Scivias* I. 4. 1; *HB* 109–10.
[19] Psalm 110:7.

and wine. The rings on their fingers were splendid, and the crosses on their gleaming red gowns. The expenses of church building, the Crusade, the emperor, the pope, the unrest of the times. The rolls of the writing, yes, those they will take with them to Trier. As growing grass becomes hay, so also you, with all your works of art, will wither, and people will walk over you as over the worst filth of the road. You have really not yet sifted through the words of reason. You jump like a grasshopper, first here, then there. You are thrown about like snow flurries. You have not yet tasted a crumb of the food of wisdom, nor have you tasted the drink of discretion. Your life is like that of birds without nest or home. Mold and ashes cling closely to you, and nowhere will you ever find rest.

Hildegard drew the bearskin up to her chin, her back stiff as a statue's. There sits the pope, clothed in purple and gold chains and rings. A homeless person. A stranger. A strand of wet hair hangs on his forehead. So much money, so many failures. He should read the writing. So many dead for nothing. The men who fail to return, the weeping women, the deprived children. And he should read this writing. His legs are heavy, but he should not stand up, he should read. That is difficult. Now and then a verb is moved ahead of its place, and the heavens open. That is exhausting. Moreover, heaven and earth are continually mingling with one another, that is hard to understand. The sapphire-blue figure in the sparkling red fire, the crystal shoes, the shining wall, the tower, the columns, the wall of light, the wings, the devil's booth. He forgets the dead, the widows and orphans, forgets that he must be on his way and cannot be where he ought to be. Suffering clay. Pilgrim in the shadow of death.

Humanity in the center of the world edifice, what it does penetrates the universe. The armor of creation. Growing grass will become hay. "A feather was touched so that it might fly up into wonders. And a strong wind bears it so that it might not sink down."[20] Her back like that of a statue, the bear-

---

[20] *Briefwechsel,* 31.

skin cannot melt it. The pope reads, there is a brightness above the bridge of his nose, not very bright, but light, lighter than he knows.

> A gem is lying in the road. But a bear comes, sees the exquisite stone, lifts its paw to take it up and place it in its lap. Then an eagle shoots down, seizes the gem, covers it with its wings and bears it through the bounds of the royal palace. Now the gem shines lustrously before the eyes of the king. He is enflamed with love for it. He gives the eagle golden shoes and praises it loudly for its cleverness.[21]

The bear trots back into the forest, not looking around. She follows it with her eyes, warmth in her hand. Moisture on her face. Anyone who is excessively fearful should place the fur on his or her breast until warmed by it. In this way, the fear will be banished. The gem, the eagle, the feather borne by the wind so it does not sink. He will drink from the stream by the path; therefore he will lift up his head.

After such nights it could be as late as Prime before Hildegard had recovered her equilibrium, dissolved the tension from her back and feet, while along the cloister walk her attempts to walk lightly still failed and despite redoubled efforts her hands were still clumsy in their care of the sick. She preferred then to go into the kitchen to clean the hearts from the chickens Wincldis had plucked and drawn, or she sat in a corner and pulled the strings from the beans, still humming the psalms. But that seldom happened. Ordinarily she was fully occupied with the sick and with her rounds, knowing that Volmar would be waiting after Terce.

Just write:

> Oh, why are you so foolish, you who are made in the image and likeness of God? How could such a great glory and honor as are given to you remain untested, as if they were idle and

---

[21] Ibid., 32.

insignificant? Gold must be refined in the fire, precious stones must be purified and polished, and all such things must be tested in every way. Therefore, you foolish people, shall that which is made in the image and likeness of God be able to endure without testing? Certainly not. The human being must be examined more than any other creature.[22]

The little girl without father and mother, she thought, who goes out, gives away her dolls, her curls, her dress, but the stars remain in heaven. We should find another conclusion— oh, Gimbert. More than any other creature, the human must be tested.

And then came the reply from Bernard of Clairvaux.

> Brother Bernard, called Abbot of Clairvaux, prays for his beloved sister in Christ Hildegard, if the prayer of a sinner may avail anything. Although you appear to think far differently of our littleness than our conscience esteems itself, we believe we should value this because of your humility alone. Yet I have in no way wished to neglect to respond to the letter of your love, even though the pressure of business forces me to reply more briefly than I would like. We rejoice with you over the grace of God that is in you. And as far as we are concerned, we caution and implore you that you regard it as grace and respond to it with the whole loving power of humility and surrender. For you know that "God resists the proud, but gives grace to the humble." Beyond this, what shall we teach or admonish, when there already exists an inner instruction and an anointing that teaches all things? Instead, we pray and urgently demand that you remember us before God and also all those who are bound with us in spiritual community in God.[23]

"You are the eagle who looks to the sun." Hildegard had to smile. Read it all again, she said to Volmar, and read slowly. The letter of your love, the pressure of business, caution and implore, the loving power of humility, grace. The

[22] *Scivias* I. 2. 29; *HB* 86-87.
[23] *Briefwechsel*, 27.

154

human being must be tested more than any other creature. The paths are not prepared for the flight to the mountain of myrrh. The stars cry out, for the moon is running away. It is a good letter, said Volmar, right and true. And Hildegard nodded.

And then, one day, the gentlemen came again, with a still greater train. Their cloaks bring wind and coolness inside; the corridor is narrow. They are thirsty. The ride was tedious, fallen trees blocked the way, there were a lot of toads, the roads are in bad condition. The mastic tree, the holm oak, Susanna in the bath, why is she thinking of these things? Hildegard is called: you should have seen it, the archbishop, eighteen cardinals, bishops from the lands of every lord sitting together, and the pope himself acting as reader, reading clearly but not too loud. The restlessness was stilled, the restlessness of hands, of crosses, one of them seems to be wrinkling up his nose, his mouth, but the pope goes on reading, as if his voice were being borne out of itself, his face is bright as he looks around.

St. Bernard stands up: such a beaming light dare not be covered by silence, and all agree with him. Here is the pope's letter, he acknowledges your writing before all the world and for all the world. Hildegard is sure of his blessing. She is a feather borne by the wind so that she may not sink down. The gentlemen offer congratulations, the sisters weep, Richardis's eyebrows gleam, mirror of the moon's path, Volmar's ears are red, big red ears. Abbot Kuno looks as if he himself had written the book. Recognition before all the world and for all the world. The sun cannot harm you by day, nor the moon by night.

Hildegard sits with Volmar. Light flows over them both. It is a lovely time, when the myrrh tree blooms. She speaks and he writes, places an object farther forward so that it can stand alone and shine. The displacement of a single verb can open the heavens. Sapphire-blue figure.

The darkness of the night no longer rises. It is the unconquerable day. The earth appears without blemish. The restless circling of sun, moon and stars has ceased. The darkness of night has been banished, and no gloom arises any more. It is the remaking of the ages. There is no more need of a light kindled by human beings. No darkness will follow. It is unchanging day.[24]

You should start again at the darkness. No, said Hildegard, anyone with sharp ears can hear with an inward sense. But Volmar shakes his head. Then you put it together, says Hildegard softly. And she slips from her chair, lays her hands on Volmar's shoulders and her forehead on his, the tips of their noses touch. It is a lovely time, when the myrrh tree blooms.

[24] Cf. *Scivias* III. 12. 15-16; HB 520-21.

In the center
of the world edifice,
the human being
a pilgrim
abducted
to foreign lands.
Burying
the remains
of the dove.
Patiently awaiting
the remaking
of the light.

XV

The Staff

Now she had to go to Ingelheim. She did not know whether this was still to be traced to King Conrad, who, shaken by storms and whirlwinds, had once sought her help; she did not know what his nephew wanted from her. She was fearful of riding and of the encounter, but she had not refused the request.

Six men in armor, their leader skillful and reticent, a sky that began to lighten from the depths upward, morning clouds, rising birds, an eagle: she tasted the air, drank the wind. A youth and a young woman, no, at thirty one is no longer a youth; what does he want? Empire and Church in tension, an effeminate age, injustice destroys justice in the vineyard, godless meddlers with anointing, lukewarm and thoughtless. The wealth of the Church was being thrown away, the spiritual order torn by wolves, driven from house and homeland. Shall a masculine age now arise? What could she do about it? She could have sung, but the bumpiness of the road, the nervous horse, the noise of the birds, the darkening sky, the excited hounds, stiffness in her limbs.

Then she saw Ingelheim, farmsteads and, behind the trees, the three towers of the chapel, moss growing on its roof. They open the gate, lead her horse to the villa, lift her down: he appears at the door, and her heart stumbles. His figure is well-balanced, his face young. Friedrich takes Hildegard's hands and bows over them; his hair smells of almonds. Of course she is hungry and thirsty, she has eaten nothing but air, drunk nothing but wind, feasted on the clouds. A small table with two chairs would have been preferable to this board with so many people around it. He has a clear brow, she thought, a mouth well suited to laughter and to ruling, his hands are lovely. She eats gladly of the pigeons' eggs, hot bread, pheasant heart with nuts and apples, drinks a cup of wine. What a long time they take over eating and drinking.

Now they are alone, Hildegard and the imperial man. The

daylight blurs beyond the windows; a beam of light steals inside and binds them together for an instant. Then Friedrich rises from his chair and kneels before Hildegard. She permits it, smells again the almond fragrance of his hair, places her hands on his shoulders. I am afraid, afraid of the burden they will lay upon me, afraid of my own power, my excessive power. Take away my fear. That I cannot do; the fear will help you to be on guard against yourself. She sees it flame up in his eyes. Hands on his shoulders, spinning in a circle and making oneself prisoner within the whirling. But she speaks of times that are as thoughtless as hussies, of the vineyards smoking with suffering, of mixers and dealers in salves.[1]

> Listen: a man stood on a high mountain, looked down into the valleys and observed what everything in them was doing. He held a staff in his hand and administered everything justly, so that what was desiccated grew green, and what was sleeping awoke.

Hildegard sees the proud mouth, the coolly burning eyes.

> The staff also took the burden of apathy from those who found themselves in great torpor. But when the man failed to open his eyes, there came a black mist that covered the valleys. Ravens and other birds tore everything roundabout asunder.[2]

Do you know, oh king, what torpor is? And do you know the opposite concepts? You must bear them, conquer restless and wild morals, and do it with mercy; you must seize your office rightly, in order that no complaint will be made against you and you must not blush for shame. Your beard will grow, she thought, red and redder, yellow and grey. Be a good servant to God, she said softly. And then she ends this conversation interrupted by silences, in which much was thought

---

[1] "Chrism makers" (*pigmentarii*) was an expression Hildegard used frequently to refer to bishops and priests. See Mother Columba Hart, "Translator's Note," *HB*, 55.

[2] See Fox, ed., *Book of Divine Works*, Letter Seven, 289.

out in advance, much anticipated; she jumps up, a little too light of foot, and kisses the king's mouth. And he laughs, takes her arm and goes down into the courtyard with her, seven steps up, seven steps down. And when Hildegard is seated on the horse, he himself hands her the parting cup.

One can always write letters, she says, and waves to him. I will write to you when you are emperor, and when you do not keep the peace and do not root out apathy and forget that you are a servant. But by that time she had already left the courtyard. The corners of his mouth are without bitterness; he has a clear brow, she will write to him before bitterness becomes fixed on him, before darkness arises. She smells the almond scent of his hair. It is good to live in this world. The horse was restless, soon began to trot, dropped back to a walk, made efforts to break into a gallop. Hildegard kept the rein tight. Had the parting cup made her dizzy?

It was quickly growing dark, because the sky was clouded over. Magpies whizzed around the baggage train and were driven away. What can they steal from me? Young eyes full of courage, cool and burning, a mouth for ruling and for laughter. O Barbarossa, Barbarossa, don't let your beard get too red, and not too long and thick, so that there may be no complaint against you. So that you need not blush for shame, servant of God.

When Hildegard arrived at the monastery it was nearly midnight. Mechthild was at the gate. Hiltrud is sick, she said, I have to tell you even though you are tired. Go to sleep now, and sleep quickly. She went to Hiltrud without taking off her travelling cloak, felt her hot forehead, her hands that seemed pulsing with fever, sat down beside her, laid one hand on her brow and the other on her hands, and remained sitting there. The sister's face looked strange in the flickering light of the candle. People are eagles and doves. A marriage of black and blue. I will make your enemies your footstool. Drink from the stream by the path. He raises up the poor from the dust, and lifts the needy from the ash heap. It is well with those who deal generously.[3] Do you know what torpor is? Remove them from apathy into blessedness, discipline and courage. Volmar will have to make some notes tomorrow about this day. Drink from the book on the way. I will make your enemies your footstool. The beard glowed in the sun, caught sparks and yet did not burn.

The bell for Matins was roaring at her. Hildegard shook the stiffness from her limbs, woke Hiltrud. Stand up, you are well. They get sick when I am away and are healthy when I am here, she thought. Too bad there was no alleluia today, she would have liked it.

[3] Psalm 110:1; 113:7; 112:5.

Jonathas

Y ou will tread on the lion and the adder, the young lion and the serpent you will trample under foot.[4]

Jonathas was like a rich and fruitful soil that is easily turned up by the plow and, when plowed, regularly brings forth useful plants; in his bearing he was calm, and in his judgments, which were true and just, he showed himself to be without hatred or anger. A person with such a character, whose essence is well distributed throughout, no matter what the diet, in the brain, the vessels and the marrow, is healthy and of an ideal constitution; in such persons anger, sadness, and conflicting moods find no soil, because God's grace is with them and, like the dew on the fields, makes them to sprout and grow green. But those who are ill with melancholy are like hard earth that can only be turned with great difficulty by the plow; in their thoughts they are full of anger, sorrow and internal contradiction. For when they are unable to pull themselves

[4] Psalm 91:13.

together through the power of their own souls, they can have no joy in their own deeds. But those with the former attitude are contented in all their works: their food causes them to increase in flesh and blood, and to be strengthened. So it was with Jonathas, whose eyes had formerly been dimmed by physical suffering, but became sharp and clear again when he was strengthened by partaking of the honey that derived its particular power from the air surrounding him.[5]

You will tread on the lion and the adder, the young lion and the serpent you will trample under foot. Hildegard sang the alleluia to herself as she was going out of the chapel. She was eager for the new day.

A great many sick were standing at the gate, come from far away. They had spent the night in the crofts and on the roadsides; they waited. Bent backs, flayed skin, enflamed nails and eyes, stinking throats, splintered teeth. Shattered by anger, wrapped up in sorrow. Come! I will wash your skin, your hair. Come! The thorn is tender, the puss runs out, I will put powdered salmon on your teeth. Come, I will rub your back with jay ointment. Go into the kitchen; they have heron hearts ready for you. Scrub out your huts, put in fresh straw, wash your clothes!

They treat their own bodies worse than they do their animals. They are stupid and have no trust in themselves. Probably in the morning they take a sip of water and spit it out as if it were poison, instead of rinsing their teeth. They take a laxative, but they do not warm themselves beforehand; they go back to work again immediately, eat cheese and raw fruit and drink water afterward, and they are not healthy. They do not realize that healing takes time, time and abstinence; they have no patience. They would not treat an animal the way they treat their own bodies. I will have to soften that in water, scour it with a stone, dry it in the sun. Come! Shattered by hatred and anger: speak. He tortures me, he hunts me, he throws chicken shit in my face, cowflaps, I am going

[5] *Heilkunde,* 282.

164

to cut his throat and gouge out his eyes. Scream it out, and then be quiet. Put your face in my hands. Rolled up in sorrow, sick as hard ground that can only be turned with difficulty. Come, sleep.

> The movement of the rational soul and the work of the body with its five senses, which compose the whole human person, have an equal weight: since the soul does not move the body to more than it can do, and the body does not accomplish any more than that to which it is stimulated by the soul, nor can the understanding separate itself from this functional circle. In this way they hold together in greater power; above and below, they enlighten the whole person for every kind of work.[6]

Jonathas was calm in his demeanor, his judgments were without hatred or anger, he is strengthened by honey, his eyes are clear, he is full of contentment in all his works. We really need a larger room for the sick, said Hildegard to the sisters, we must pray harder. For God will command the angels to guard you in all your ways. On their hands they will bear you up, lest you dash your foot against a stone. You will tread on the lion and the adder, the young lion and the serpent you will trample under foot.[7]

After None there was a letter with the archbishop's seal. Hildegard was frightened. Read, said she to Volmar. It was about a journey that Hildegard was to undertake. Who am I to do that? I, a woman. Aloud she said that she needed time to think, and more precise information. Everything is here, said Volmar: places, times, number of sermons. There are eyes and ears to be opened; it is a question of conversion. These are restless and godless times. No delay can be tolerated. Tread on lions and vipers. The angels, the angels. Read it all again, slowly, said Hildegard. What is your advice? It is a duty, said Volmar, but the physical strains. . . . To hang

[6] Ibid., 281.
[7] Psalm 91:11-13.

on your ears when I know not how to go on, to lay my forehead against yours, but not even a stone could break out
through the grilled window. Tread on serpents and adders.
You must decide, the messenger is waiting. I need time.

Hildegard stood up and went into the garden. I have no
cloak and no shoes, only the ordering of the time from Matins
to Compline and a bearskin at night. She put her hands in
her sleeves, felt her bones, her chafed skin, put one foot in
front of the other, smelled the smoky air, was it so late that
the farmers were already burning the weeds, was Clementia
taking care that they got the ashes? The harvest of apples and
pears and beets, the winepress for the grapes, the grinding
of the grain. The sisters. The sick. Mechthild? The water in
the well was gray, like the sky.

We are like birds who stare at their reflections in the water
and, since they are aware of nothing else, soon die. Restless
and godless are the times. Conversion. Is that my office? God
will command the angels to guard you in all your ways. On
their hands they will bear you up, lest you dash your foot
against a stone. You will tread on the lion and the adder, the
young lion and the serpent you will trample under foot. The
bell rings for Vespers. Criseldis, let the plectrum cry. Steps,
gestures, words, breath: bound and formed. Yes, that is easy.
The angels, the angels. Lest you dash your foot against a stone.
Alas, the lions, the adders.

After Vespers, Hildegard presented the case to the sisters.
Resistance, murmuring, flashing eyes. What are you going
to do out in the world? Since when do you doubt the power
of prayer? Obedience to whom? They got no farther. Why
did she not decide, clearly and definitely, this way or that?
The clamps in her legs, the screws in her back, the nails driven
into her toes, her teeth pegged. Then she told Volmar to send
the messenger back with her assent. May the world not break
into your dreams, she said to the sisters, and went to the sick.
She took the soaked bandage from the farm wife's head and
saw that her eyes had become clear. It is all quite simple, she
said; the bandage must only be allowed to do its work for three

days. Sleep one more night, and early tomorrow we will wash your hair. Then you may go home. Be happy. She sat down on the trunk by the girl and stroked until her sobbing ceased. *O frondens virga, in tua nobilitate stans, sicut aurora procedit. Nunc gaude et laetare et nos debiles dignare a mala consuetudine liberare, atque manum tuam porrige ad erigendum nos.*[8] She hummed.

Every element has its sound, an original sound by God's command; all these tones join like the harmony of harps and zithers. This unified sound of heaven, however, does not extend to that harmony of the elements that are exchanged with human beings. And yet. . . . Since a human being often sighs and groans on hearing a song, since she or he is reminded of the nature of the heavenly harmony of souls, we are compelled to sing and praise. All arts that serve the useful and necessary desires of human beings are the inventions of the living breath of God. This shipwrecked world. The human being, the stranger. Compelled to sing and praise. The girl looked wonderingly at Hildegard. I will go home, and I will not kill my father; I will take care of him. Yes, said Hildegard, and now sleep, I will stay by you a little while. Already she saw new figures approaching in the morning grayness, beggars before the Lord. Chase away your sadness. There are angels that bear you on their hands. Bring water from the river, wash yourselves with stones, hang your souls in the sun, air out your rooms, *o frondens virga, in tua nobilitate stans,*[9] be rich and fruitful ground that is easily turned by the plow and repeatedly, when plowed, brings forth useful plants The honey is strong because of the air around it.

All the arts are the invention of the living breath of God. Hildegard took her bearskin, sat down on it, and wrapped herself in her habit. Brother, dear brother, she said, but she did not know why she said it. Duty or not, I will see, trample

[8] "O leafy branch, standing in your nobility as the dawn breaks forth: now rejoice and be glad, and deign to set us frail ones free from evil habits and stretch forth your hand to lift us up." *Symphonia* II. 15.

[9] Ibid.

on young lions, tread on dragons. I will have no fear before men and women. This shipwrecked world. This stranger, the human being. Easily turned by the plow, this Jonathas, calm in his bearing, true and just in his judgments, always bringing forth useful plants. Ah, Jonathas. The clear eyes. The air has given strength to the honey. On light feet you walk over lions and adders. *Nunc gaude et laetare et nos debiles dignare a mala consuetudine liberare.*[10] Godless. I have no cloak and no shoes.

[10] Ibid.

Salt Marsh and Wasteland

I have established the firmament with all its array, and it lacks for nothing. It has all these: eyes for seeing, ears for hearing, the nose for smelling and the mouth for tasting. For the sun is like the light of the eyes, the wind like the hearing of the ears, the air like smelling and the dew that rises from the greening is like the breath of the mouth. And the moon indicates the time of the tides and is an indication of human knowledge. The stars in their courses reveal a certain reason, as reason is able on the whole to grasp certain things. In four ways have I made fast the corners of the world: with fire, clouds and water, in order to knit together all the ends of the earth as with veins. The stones I have moistened with fire and water like bones, and the earth have I made fast with moisture and greenness, like the marrow of the living organism.[11]

Her voice was soft and clear, lifting only a little at the comma, sinking at the period, sentence by sentence.

[11] Hildegard of Bingen, *Gotteserfahrung, und Weg in die Welt,* ed. Heinrich Schipperges (Olten and Freiburg: Walter, 3d ed. 1980) 191. Cited hereafter as *Gotteserfahrung.*

Even so, her breathing threatened to crush itself together and cut off her air. Breathe deeper, speak more slowly, leave time for the final syllables. Pause from time to time. Fix the contours of the figures, look into one or another of the faces.

> Thus everything is fixed and fast, and nothing is lacking. For if the clouds lacked fire and water, they would collapse like dust. And if the other stars did not take their light from the sun, they could not sparkle through the water; they would be blind. All these are also the tools for the bodily construction of human beings, who can understand in touching, kissing and embracing how everything is at their disposal in their contact with the world, in whose company human beings are accustomed to exercise their honorable office. For if human beings were not capable of everything, the world could not be their partner. But in this way the world lives with human beings, and human beings live in and with it. [12]

She stopped for a moment, then repeated the sentence about partnership and the one after it. Her breathing had found its depth and rhythm, so that she could reduce her volume a little without her voice's losing its clarity. She saw the glow of the purple robes, the golden chains, the sparkling of the rings: why are you not ashamed when you realize that all the other creatures do not neglect the commandments, but fulfill them, while your tongues are dumb. You do not desire holy reason, which has its own course like that of the stars. You are night, and you breathe darkness, a stubborn and decayed people that, in its great contentment, no longer walks in the light. As a naked snake creeps into its hole, so you go around in the stench of the lower animals. And yet you should be the mountain, the place of God's dwelling.

But that is just what you are not. You look only to what you yourselves have produced, and you approve of all deeds according to your own opinion. You do this and neglect that, just as it pleases you. Come to your senses, deliver yourselves

[12] Ibid., 192.

from being forgotten by God. Stop wounding your souls and failing yourselves. She wanted to repeat those two sentences, sought for another formulation, was silent. Er-high, er-high! Ludger gave her a mighty shove. Er-high? Er-high! And the pine trees bent. Nough-e, nough-e, but then she swung over the top, and before her heart could recover, the swift fall. Falling like birds without wings. Nough-e! Nough-e. But Ludger sat on her dolls' church tower and laughed. Like birds without wings, falling. But a feather flies, miraculously, upward, And a strong wind bore her, so that she might not sink down.

Talking, being with them. Looking into their faces. Putting her hands in her sleeves, listening. Looking into their faces, grey with care, twisted by doubt, fat with good living. Listening. The times for sleeping are lengthened, time at table extended, bathing periods multiplied, divine services shortened. They are incapable of any kind of asceticism. What for? The food tastes good, the wine is tasty. Eating and drinking keep body and soul together. Looking into their faces, shining with well-being, in their twinkling eyes. Asceticism, what for? You only live once. Godlessness. Devastation, neglect, despondency and failure. Listening. Stop falling short of what you are. "Collect yourself now, so that your heart may not blaze up in that softness that, through the instability of worldly life, will do you great harm. But you should live, for God's grace desires you."[13]

Do you know what that means: you should live, for grace— listen carefully—the grace of God desires you. "Therefore beware lest you withdraw from it in the wilful wandering of your spirit."[14] What is asceticism? You must not withdraw. Talking. Listening. Hands in the sleeves. Looking into their eyes. And then silence, dropping the eyes, the countless candles shine so brightly, the red-gold cups glisten, the silver bowls, the towers of fruit, the blue trout, the fat capons garnished with cherries, stuffed with truffles and roasted almonds,

[13] *Briefwechsel,* 211.
[14] Ibid.

surrounded by golden goose eggs, the white bread, the sugared cakes. Hildegard sees the sparkling rings, a double chin, the white lips, the waving linen napkins, hears the smacking and slurping and gurgling and swallowing. Eat a little meat, a cherry, break off a piece of bread, drink from the red-gold cup. Don't look at Volmar or at Hiltrud. Pick up the red and blue sugar in your fingers, the bits fallen from the cake. The lights flicker on the shining mouths, the red faces. It is late. Good night.

Hiltrud lays her forehead on Hildegard's knee and weeps. Are you thinking of Jutta and St. Disibod? Hiltrud nodded: let's turn back, plow the dry ground at Rupertsberg and clear it of stones. Say that you are not up to it. No, said Hildegard, I will not turn back, I am equal to it, I must know how things look in the world. Shall I roll up my life like a weaver?[15] Hiltrud grew quiet and fell asleep. Hildegard let her arms hang down and closed her eyes. I will not weep, not yet. She felt the rocking pace of the horse, the slipping of its feet on the stones. I have not tasted the air, smelled the wind, or seen even a patch of sky, only the twig that, if the servant had not been paying attention, would have whipped across my face, only the grotesque faces of the hounds at the side of the road, the masks of the staring people. As if she could roll up her life like a weaver. Twisted into a ball and thrown away. Falling like birds without wings. Nothing but falsity. Failure of the self, spoiled by selfishness.

The darkness makes the stomach heavy and the heart stubborn. Eyes and ears of a donkey. Obstinate people, spoiled, in their well-being no longer walking in the light. Gluttony, thirst for glory, passion for finery and possessions. Pride, envy, and hate. Serpents in the darkness. The human being, the powerful human being, the mighty partner of the world. Sweep the plunder aside! A ship sails through the inn, silver and round as a bowl, a ship without masts, without sail; it crunches on the sand. The floods. The floods.

[15] Isaiah 38:12.

171

Hildegard awoke right on time, at two o'clock, felt her way through the house, found the chapel. She had not wakened Hiltrud, she did not wait for Volmar. The eternal light burned. I have a portion in land and cup, fair to me is my inheritance. I give you my life as booty in all places. Fair to me is my inheritance. I will not fall like a bird without wings.[16] But then she covered her face with her hands. I will not weep, not yet. She was still. Later, Volmar came, and Hiltrud also. They sang Lauds as usual. When the dawn came, they could hear steps. Someone went hastily to the altar. Every movement was exact, every word articulated. It was memorized. Not mechanical, but with virtuosity, rapid, glib. Others had entered the room, like puppets, voiceless. In twenty minutes it was all over. No communion, no community in prayer. But not a word or a gesture was lacking, everything was indicated, everything said. Elegant as a lizard. Hildegard was wide awake. Twenty minutes, if she was not mistaken, at the most. A Mass. *Ite, missa est. Deo gratias.*[17]

Hello and good morning, breakfast is ready. But when Hildegard tried to excuse herself, there was Hugo standing before her. He took her on his arm and turned with her in a circle. Come, sister, I am hungry. He had been on a journey, and had had to make detours because of the dangers. But now he was here. You are dry and wrinkled, sister, come! Eating and drinking keeps body and soul together. Brother, dear brother, how lovely it is to see you, brother, dearest brother. But she said nothing. Hildegard saw the rings on his fingers, his polished nails, his golden chain. He must certainly eat and drink after such a journey full of fear and false turnings, and he must also make himself splendid, that is the way it is. Her glance stole to his eyes, and she was happy, drank the almond milk, took a little piece of chicken breast on her bread, while Hugo turned his attention to the goose's leg and forgot the sisters.

[16] Cf. Psalm 16:5-6.
[17] Go, the Mass is finished. Thanks be to God.

Brother, said Hildegard softly, you all drink too much and eat too much, your tables are groaning. But Hugo heard nothing, and Hildegard had probably spoken too gently. She saw his powerful chest. Like their father's. His shoulders, too, and his neck up to his ears. Brother. But their father's hands had been longer and more slender. Walking, admiring the gardens, the rosebushes, the Chinese oak, the hedges cut into shapes like bulls, the pond with the fountain; talking about traveling, the crusade, the dangers, the treasures, about buildings and people, eating and drinking, viewing the municipal fountain, the community house, the streets; faces moved rapidly before her eyes, the perfumes of Arabian oils rose to her nostrils, garments rustled and whispered, rings bit into Hildegard's hand.

> Your spirits are like clouds pregnant with storm: first they surrender wearily to slothful anger, then they submit to beastly filth. You say: we are unwilling to oppose our own natures, for we cannot gird the loins of our bodies. Why are you not ashamed, you who have been rescued from the asses' stable by the most high Lord and placed in honorable service, to run like idiots back to the asses' stall? Oh, alas! In this you are like Balaam, who, mad from wounds and burning slashes, took his repose in the land of the shadow of death. Do not abandon the mountain.[18]

For God loves humanity very much. Preaching. Talking. Hearing. Listening. Talking.

> Your spiritual attitude is like a slumber. I see in you a fruitless inclination to slumber and forgetfulness. Wipe from the eyes of your hearts the restlessness of your spirits and shake off your sadness. Why do you not beat the worthless servants who secretly pester you like stinging spiders? Now the time has come for the battle over people's way of life, since they stand neither in discipline nor in the strictness of the fear of God.[19]

[18] *Briefwechsel*, 126-27. See Fox, ed., *Book of Divine Works*, Letter Sixteen: Hildegard to the Monks of Zwiefalten, 305-06.
[19] *Briefwechsel*, 130-31.

Preaching, talking, hearing, talking, putting her hands in the sleeves of her habit, being silent. Sometimes Hildegard succeeded in taking a few men with her into the chapel or the church; sometimes it was a hundred. And when she sang in the deadly silence and Hiltrud and Volmar added their voices, it could happen that a fourth and a fifth voice joined them. We have escaped like a bird from the snare of the fowlers; the snare is broken, and we have escaped. We have escaped like a bird from the snare of the fowlers.[20] Eared owls and ravens, fools and knaves. Alas. Sweep aside the plunder. Be converted.

No matter whether men or women. They live for the day, said Bilhildis, safe and well served, weaving for show, embroidering things that are never finished; they have reduced the divine services to three half-hours, and for the most part they skip them because they are not in the mood, they gobble and drink, they are lethargic, fat and dull, but it is my fault, I know it. She wept; the blue bags under her eyes jiggled. Help us! Hildegard was silent; she took the sister by the hand and went with her into the garden. Odor of asters and nuts. Dragonflies hovering. Overgrown bushes, wilted rose hips, wildly growing weeds in the beds and on the paths, withered apples and quinces in which wasps were buzzing; a hedgehog was sleeping under the leaves in the well.

I should take the silk dresses from these ladies, give them hair shirts and chase them into the garden, thought Hildegard, until they are so tired they can no longer eat their eel paté and their roast venison and cannot swallow their wine. I should pull their down pillows from their beds and sweep their tables bare. But she said nothing, held Bilhildis's hand, looked, sniffed, breathed. Brought to the point of withering and despairing of life. What should she do? Pull yourself together now, so that your heart may not blaze with that softness that, through the instability of worldly life, will do you great harm. But you should live, because the grace of God desires you.

[20] Psalm 124:7.

Take care, then, not to withdraw from it in the wandering of your spirit. This she said softly. But she knew that she was talking to the wind. Brought to the point of withering and despairing of life. They went back into the house. Hildegard called the ladies together and began to tell of St. Rupert in the shipwrecked world, this friend of God who built a church and founded a settlement for the poor, the sinners, the lost sheep. The walls of living stones sparkled, flying high in heaven like clouds through the zeal of their good will. And he in their midst, unstained nor swallowed by the dance in the old cave, nor weakened by the wounds inflicted by the old enemy. The Holy Spirit sang and played in him. A vessel of beauty. Entirely made up of longing. She told of her building.

> For a time my eyes were darkened, and I could no longer see any light. I felt my body pressed down by such a weight that I could not lift myself up, and I lay thrown down by powerful pains. This I suffered until I acknowledged the place where I now live.[21]

She told of the months of tension and struggle, of the rage of the demons. She told of the wilderness locale with no human neighbors to help, without the barest necessities of life, of cold, hunger, the murmuring of the sisters who left her, the hard work in house and garden, conquering the earth arduously, yard by yard. She lifted her voice a little at the end of the sentence, noting how strength was drawn out of her along with her voice, but she did not stop in the telling. She concluded softly: I am the life, I am the fully sound life; not carved from stones, not blooming from twigs, not rooted in the procreative power of the man. Sapphire-blue figure. Go now, reflect. God desires you all.

The journey continued, from city to city, from monastery to monastery, week after week. Listening, talking, listening, being silent, at night putting her face in her hands. I am the

[21] Gronau, 182–83.

life, the fully sound life. Sapphire-blue. They are wounding their souls. They are false to themselves, they are falling like birds without wings, rolling up their lives like a weaver. The sun is ashamed, the moon blushes. You are pregnant with hay and you will bring forth straw. Dry land full of broken thorn bushes. Fools and knaves. Wound into a ball and thrown away.

At night, her face is in her hands. Not to let oneself be overcome by anger, not to spit it out, not to let oneself be seized by rage; shaken by weeping. Chrism makers. Effeminate people. Effeminate age. Have you never heard of the sevenfold light of the sun? I will not turn away from the fragile earth, but will fight valiantly against it. Shaken by weeping.

When she returned to Rupertsberg, winter had begun.

Oscillation

The tenth month is like a seated person. It no longer hastens forward swiftly in the full power of its greening freshness of life, and it no longer possesses the fullness of living warmth. Instead, it decorates the foliage of the trees by sweating the cold out of it. In the same way, the seated person gathers him- or herself together to avoid the cold. One puts on a garment in order to be warm. This is an example of the fact that human beings, when they grow old and begin to freeze, are also wiser. For, sated with childish morals, a person in the ripeness of age more easily curbs inconstancy and foolish behavior. Such a one avoids the company of stupid people who would only deceive with their ignorance. Moreover, because of the coldness of age, the manifold and now superfluous desires of the flesh recede. And so it is also true that this month, despite all its greening power, is no longer entirely pleasant, since as a result of the dryness and cold the branches lose their leaves.

But the soul, created as a living and intelligent breath of
the Spirit of God, who in truth is Wisdom itself, teaches
human beings to hold fast to what comes from God. With
God's grace, the soul in a blessed person submits itself to the
body, together with all its powers, as the handmaid to her
mistress, and gives it joy in what is good. But when the flesh
of this person should again be aroused by a lust for pleasure,
the soul is indignant and amazed, sucks that poison out of
the vessels and the marrow and puts an end to it. She con
soles the body with the grace of the Holy Spirit and the teach-
ings of Holy Scripture, leads it from vice to virtue so that it
may not be destroyed by sin, and so takes it carefully under
her protection.[22]

After every journey there is the joy of Rupertsberg, the
bright faces, Hildegard's voice with new notes from
Matins to Compline. I have a share in land and cup, fair to
me is my inheritance.[23] Volmar's big ear. The words. The
sayings. The singing of the slate pencil. In the ripeness of age
one curbs inconstancy and avoids the company of stupid
people. The salve dealers, the effeminate nation. Clementia's
storehouse is filled with dried herbs, powders, and pastes. The
perennials in the garden are covered with mulch. In the cel-
lars there are beets and beans, oats and barley, pears and
apples. The pelts of the sheep are growing. The bearskin
warms her at night. Without mast or sails is the hull, but the
river soon fills its bending course. The floods have lifted up
their voices; may the floods lift up their roaring.[24] The water
has fifteen powers, the meadows glide away, the vineyards
approach, the dock wavers. Hugo's hair smells of Arabian
oil; he has diamonds in his ear. Come, brother, come into
the hollow tree; I will weave you a rope of rushes. Don't listen to the hunting horn; stay here, royal hunts. Richardis
comes through the forest with swaying hips, a golden train.
She mounts a horse and rides away, her gown balloons

[22] *De operatione Dei* I. 4. 98.
[23] Psalm 16:5-6.
[24] Psalm 93:3.

proudly, hair waves about her missing eye, to the dance in the ancient cave, past the chains of the people, the dogs, the cats, the faces with blue bags. The hem of my skirt has come loose; it is dragging through the mud. Hugo is bringing roasted hedgehog on a platter, its spines garnished with cherries, wine is flowing through the window.

Hildegard sits up, her heart pounding. She curls up and draws the bearskin around her body. When in old age one begins to freeze, one is also wiser, curbs inconstancy, and avoids the society of stupid people. She sees the Count of Wertheim before her, amongst the corpses, the sword that he thrusts into his body, hears their cries. I am the life, the fullness of life. I did not know what I should do, says the father, but I would not let him starve and freeze, we can be happy that we were preserved from that. They should prepare a bath for him, cut his beard, give him a fur and a hot soup three times a day, says the mother. They wanted to break him. Then they are both silent. Someone had to be broken by hunger, cold, and darkness. Hildegard asks Rena, but she shakes her head; finally she learns it from Gimbert: the emperor has been captured, and his son is searching for him.

The emperor? But no one can capture an emperor and break him like a stick of wood. No one is allowed to do anything for him, says Gimbert. He will sink down in filth and be crushed in the darkness of the cellar. But he dressed himself as a monk, walked over stony paths, knelt before the pope and put his face to the ground. Yes, yes, Gimbert said; that is so. They cut the old man's tongue out and chopped off his hands, says Ratbert. But Hildegard does not believe it. I will not eat until they give the emperor something to eat. I will not cover myself as long as the emperor is freezing. But she is taught otherwise. If I were not a little girl, I would bring him a light so he would not break his forehead; I would bring him some bread. If I were bigger, I would free him. At night she lies down beside him, to warm him, and she herself becomes a stone. She ties her doll, the poor king, on her back, sits straight and stiff, leans against nothing, walks about with the doll's head banging against her neck; at night she does not untie it, but she groans under the weight. After some days, her father returns.

The emperor has publicly resigned his sceptre and staff and given the rule to his son. You can all relax. He is an old man and will soon die. His life was difficult. He did not want to submit to the Church. Why didn't he want to submit to the Church? Go to sleep! He is an old man, he will soon die, but they did not break him. Hildegard puts the doll king away, feels the light on the bridge of her nose, buries her face in the blankets. She draws the bearskin more closely about her; she sees the young Barbarossa, the chrism makers, greasy waistcoats, weeds of affluence, sees the corners of the young emperor's mouth, his clear brow. He would never put his face to the ground before the pope; his eyes burn coolly. The almond scent of his hair, the beam of light that bound them together. The fear will help you to be on the alert. The fear. She presses the bearskin against her neck. The staff also takes away the burden of dullness, extinguishes the vineyards smoking with sorrow. That you may not be accused, servant of God. Your beard is so red. I lay my hands on your shoulders.

At last the bell rang for Matins. Hildegard jumped up and shook herself. Day to day pours forth speech, and night to night declares knowledge.[25] My inheritance, my inheritance. Listen to how this sounds, said Hildegard to Volmar: *Arrezenpholianz et Kelionz,* what do you think, what if they spoke with one another surrounded by Aieganz, breathed upon by Ispariz, far from Diueliz, the Luzeia of Inimois would be bright and the Oir open. Aigonz, Aigonz. Volmar noted the strange words. But we must proceed systematically. We will begin with the objects in the house and garden, with weapons or articles of clothing, then we will go on to the herbs and fruits, to Cririscha and Briunz, to the animals, Wilischio and Balbunz and Asgriz. We must not forget the months, days, and

[25] Psalm 19:2.

seasons, until we return to Kelionz, and then we will let him speak with Perezilinz.

Hildegard was silent. She had thrust her hands deeply into her sleeves and sat there with rounded shoulders, while Volmar went on writing and tried to make the words look handsome: a rounding here, an opening there, a flourish. Yes, you are right, said Hildegard, we need a new script also. She took the board and her pencil. Let's invent an H, an I, L, D, E, and G, A, and R, each individually. Then they compared their creations and smiled at their resemblances, sought what they had in common, selected the letters that seemed better. Hildegard's eyes shone, and Volmar, when he saw it, bowed his head deeper over the board and drew it back into his hood. Often we cannot find a Latin word, he said, and now this. You are putting up barriers of language. But no, no, on the contrary, look at them all together, the Rischol, Scaltizio, Tronziol, Linschiol and Korzinthio and Morizinz. Write it all down, I will repeat it again.

The bell for Sext, the bell for None did not reach them, new words were continually pressing on her, every word formed itself anew, sounded strange, strange in its vowels and in its consonants. Dizol, Discula, Munizza, Aieziz. Write:

> I, who am without origin and the source of every beginning, I who am the ancient of days, I say: I am day in myself, a day that does not shine forth from the sun, but rather lends to the sun its flame. I am reason that is not apprehended through another, but from which all rational being draws breath. So for the perception of my face I have created mirrors in which I regard all the wonders of my originality, which never cease. I have prepared these mirror-forms for myself, that they may join in the song of praise, for I have a voice like the sound of thunder with which I hold the whole universe in motion in the living sounds of all creatures. This have I done, I, the ancient of days. Through my word that was and is in me without beginning, I send forth a mighty light, and in it are countless sparks, the angels. But when they be-

came aware of their light, they forgot me and wanted to be as I am. Therefore I rejected them.

After that I spoke within myself my little work that is the human being. This I formed according to my image and after my likeness, that it might be realized with respect to myself. I have established this work in a spiritual way according to my reason and in it I have indicated my possibility, just as the human spirit comprehends everything in its artistic capacity by name and number. In no other way than by names can the human being comprehend the essence of things, and in no other way than through number can it understand their multiplicity.[26]

Hildegard stopped and reflected. Then everything in creation came to be by a creative utterance. Borne by God's prior knowledge, everything was given its name and its own number. And in the human power of speech the likeness of God is contained. When God spoke to human beings, language was awakened within them. Write:

In the very beginning of things, God's will opened itself to the creation of nature. Without such a beginning, God would have remained alone, without revealing Godself. For the Word had no beginning at all. With this Word God willed that the Word should create everything, as it had been planned from eternity. And why was it called the Word? Because with the sound of its voice it awakened the whole creation and because it called creation to itself. So when the Word of God sounded forth, this Word appeared in every creature, and this sound was the life in every creature. The human spirit effects all its works through this same Word; by this one sound reason accomplishes its deeds in a resounding way, by shouting or singing. Thus the human being is gifted with reason according to the image of God through its living soul.[27]

In that case, said Volmar, there is an original language, and the confusion of tongues was brought about by original

[26] *De operatione Dei* I. 4. 105; see *Book of Divine Works*, 128–29.
[27] Ibid.

sin. Yes, yes, said Hildegard, but the heavenly language can be translated into every human tongue, and those are also understood in the world above. But perhaps we can remember back and tear it out of the past. Her stomach hurt. She saw that the tip of Volmar's nose was white, and she was startled. Let us take a turn in the garden. But then the bell for Vespers rang.

Scent of almonds,
eyes coolly burning,
stricken with blindness,
unholy age.
Resistance
I destroy,
those who oppose me
I grind
through my own self.
Alas
for the blasphemers
who despise me.
Your beard is growing grey.
Where is the staff?
Chrism makers
walking in a wasteland
pregnant with hay,
bringing forth straw
in the dance
in the cave.
And day calls out to day,
night to night declares knowledge:
we could speak
the language of the angels,
it would be such a delight.
Alas,
my back is stiff.

XVI

Hide me in the Shadow of Your Wings

These were good times. The light streamed unhindered into the world; it was there daily at midday, but without heat; it stood still for a moment and then withdrew. Hildegard watched the rise and fall, and the day was fulfilled. Before she saw to the sick, she embraced armfuls of light; she treated and comforted the patients and turned them over to the sisters, went into the scriptorium and began to speak even as she was entering; see, Volmar is there and ready with ear and pencil. The words came to her tongue without hesitation, and Volmar did not question, but wrote; his ear was big and open. When she turned her attention outward, she may have noticed a drop on the tip of his nose and she was glad: the wedding of labor. Dear Volmar, she must have thought then. But had his nose not grown sharper, and did it not have a bluish cast? Still, when she thought of this, her seeing was already past and she was lifted up in the speaking of the words, of the black, purple and green of wall, tower and tree, of sapphire and gown turning to blue and white and changing themselves into lion and eagle and angel.

Sometimes neither of them heard the bell, and they were brought from their work only by their empty stomachs. We should have a cup of wine and bread here, and then another cup of wine and a chicken wing, and we could go on working. But Volmar preferred a soup to the wine and said, drawing himself up wearily, that a chicken wing, tough from flying around, would be nothing for me. And so both of them went to the dining hall, looked at the others, tried to hear what the reader was saying, and noticed that their stomachs were quickly filled, and could have used a diluted wine that expands the stomach, washes down the mouthfuls, and does not make one weary.

In these weeks of transition from summer to fall, they also worked during the siesta. On his way to the scriptorium, Volmar splashed a little water from the well into his face, while

Hildegard slept for five minutes, then shook herself and asked where they had stopped. It is good to go on, one never knows what may happen. How so? What might happen? asked Hildegard: a birth, a failing heart, a rider with bad news? Read me the last thing you wrote. And Volmar read, softly and evenly. She ought to rest for a moment in this deep, lovely voice, surrender herself to its sound. And she asked Volmar to repeat a passage, saying there was a mistake in it, and she floated into it in a boat and saw the sky above her. Dear Volmar. Let us go on, and whenever I have finished a thought you must repeat what you have written, so that I can develop the next idea out of it.

> For a person who follows foolishness and despises wisdom, through which God created everything, condemns him- or herself, taking no measure of evil and regarding eternal life as nothing. Such a one does not even wish to know whether there is another life, nor to investigate closely and conscientiously what the reason is that his or her nature is so changeable. One may understand one's infancy and childhood, youth and maturity; but what will become of one after one's time has been lived out, that is something that no one can grasp at all, nor how he or she will be changed. In the rationality of the soul a person recognizes that he or she has had a beginning. But what it means to say that the soul does not die and there is no end to it, no person can in any way know or understand.[1]

Hildegard faltered. It is time for siesta, and it is not good for us to be always working, so that we can no longer feel our own legs or hear the beating of our hearts. Let us walk a little. Volmar stood up and straightened himself to walk. They exited through their individual doors, and outside in the garden they met again and sought a path that was wide enough for the two of them. Since there was no such path, they moved in a kind of dance, threading around one another, now one of them ahead, now the other; each one wanted to

[1] *De operatione Dei,* 278.

allow the other to go first and so threaded his or her way back again. Volmar could move with a little more suppleness, Hildegard found, and she began to hum a litany, but interrupted it when their habits got tangled in one another before they had completed their change of places. Thus they arrived at the garden gate, and Hildegard opened it; she wanted to turn the key but could not. Then Volmar laid his hand on hers, and they turned the key together, and when their other hands found themselves together on the handle to press it down and pull it to open the gate, they both had to smile and shrink back at the same time.

We are heroes, said Hildegard, and she did not want to hear how Volmar was wheezing. Look at the field, she said, how golden it is in the midday sun. And Volmar nodded and was still wheezing. Hildegard took tiny, slow steps, so that Volmar's breathing could grow easier. She was silent. A pain fixed itself at the base of her neck, and she would have liked to swing her arms in circles. We are old, both of us, and high spirits don't suit us. Volmar was walking beside her now, their paces matching one another, and when the skirts of their habits brushed one another they made a sound like the beating of birds' wings or the rolling of gentle waves.

Clouds of smoke. The smell of burned vegetation. The fields have been harvested. The birds' wings of their habits. Rhythm of their steps. We must not die, said Hildegard suddenly, we still have a lot to do. How much taller Volmar was than she, and she could not see anything of his face, not even the tip of his nose. Do you feel the warmth on your back? she asked. Or are you ready to die, tired of the innumerable steps and sated with prayers? We ought to have laid it aside at the same time, this life, don't you think? Now she heard Volmar's breathing again, in the midday air of the fields, composed of sun and the smoke of the grass and the weariness of the summer declining to its end. Volmar sat down on a boulder, slipped the hood from his head, and held his face up to the sun.

Hildegard stood nearby, shocked by the wet strands of hair on his head, looking at the warts on his face. Had she really removed them with her saliva, how long ago was that, that time at the well? She squatted on the ground. Her bones were old, but to squat next to Volmar in a golden field in the sun as it was bidding them farewell, that was good. And she laid her hand on his knee and forgot her thoughts of death. Not even a rabbit will see us here on the side of the path, she thought. She wanted to begin with her memories, the grill, the big ear, I am Volmar, and we will imagine the grill away; but she let it drop, what good does it do to talk? Her hand on his knee.

Soon they would walk back and lock the gate, go to prayers and take up their work again. There was still a lot to do. No one should sleep unnecessarily; the penalty is death. Come, let us go back, there is not a lark to greet us. When she leaned on his knee to push herself up, he took her wrist and pushed it upward along with her. You have cold hands; come, we will walk toward the light, that will warm you. Give me your hand. And Volmar did so, and again their habit skirts circled in and out of one another as they measured their paces to each other. Volmar locked the gate and gave Hildegard the key. Then they turned their gaze inwards and hurried to the chapel. Not a rabbit, not a lark, and his hands are cold, and I was squatting on the ground as if I were a young thing. There was something right about the scriptorium and the window that only showed his ear.

Volmar did not come at the time when work should begin. Hildegard stood at the window, waited, sent Hiltrud away, stood at the window without seeing, waited. What she had wanted to dictate vanished from her head. That night. Volmar's warm breath in her ear. The attention of the angel. I am Volmar, and we will imagine the grill away. I will hang onto to these ears when I know not how to go on. Then she did not wait any longer. The bluish tip of his nose, his wheezing breath, his cold, bony hand, his silence. There is still a lot to be done. Now what?

When the bell rang for Vespers they brought her the news

of Volmar's death. I know. She heard the beating wings of their habits, felt his hand on her wrist. Not a rabbit. Not a lark. Smell of burning. A declining summer. Her hand on his knee. The dance of their habit skirts over the mown field. The key. Her entrails are torn, her breast explodes, her throat splinters. Until Compline, Hildegard sits there, her left hand gripping her right wrist, dear Volmar, she sits there, say dear Volmar, torn, entrails, breast, throat and eyes. My speech and yours, the sound of our voices. The big ear.

Clementia takes Hildegard by the hand, leads her into the chapel and out again, takes her to her cell, removes her sandals, takes off her habit, lays the bearskin over her, gives her a sleeping draught. When Clementia has fallen asleep, Hildegard gets up softly, puts on her habit and goes into the south porch of the church. A candle is flickering beside the bier. She pushes down the wedge beneath Volmar's chin, reties the neckband, straightens the ends of the hood, sits down on the edge of the bier, pushes back a strand of hair under the hood, looks into his face for a long time, passes her middle finger over his thin eyebrows, the bridge of his nose, his lips, sits, looks at his face, renews the candle, the edge of the bier digs into her flesh. Hide me in the shadow of your wings. She lays her head on his hands. We lie well this way, we could lie here a long time, an old woman and a dead man.

St. Benedict. St. Rupert. An angel with naked wings, come, we will wash the wings with sand, reddish sand from Egypt, Volmar must look it up and see how one writes "Egypt" in Latin, he cannot find the word, pulls his hood far over his face, sprinkles sand in the angel's hair, reddish sand from Egypt. They are pulling hard on the angel, their breath is failing, you must not give up, don't leave me alone, we need the angel as a watcher for our vineyard, sweet-tasting juice, dividing roots, flickering leaf. Do not cast the eye from the eye, do not cut off the light from the light. Do you think that the reddish sand from Egypt makes the grapes blue, blue and fruity? We will put the angel here. Do not cut off the light from the light.

The Path Is Not Ready for the Flight to the Mountain of Myrrh

You must still certify the documents, says Volmar, the documents for the angel and the vineyard. Yes, yes, says Hildegard, but first I have to go north, see the furrow that leads down here and back up there, hear how the wild geese cry before it is autumn, announce the winter and how the north wind fumbles around the house, laden with cold, before the ice and snow come; I must get her, she wants to come back, I only have to take her by the hand and bring her here, only go ahead of me, everything down there tastes of salt: the water, the trees, the grasses. Wild geese are crying day and night, take the staff, go ahead of me, always along this furrow. But Volmar shakes his head: they have also given us a stretch of river, you have to certify that, too.

Yes, yes, said Hildegard, there is sturgeon in it; when its bones are burned the spirits depart, and the salmon's flesh is soft and powerless like the moon, it is always swimming in the moonlight, always, but first we have to go north and get her. I am a pilgrim in the shadow of death, like ashes and floating dust, O child, beloved child, where are the forecourts of heaven, alas for the flight to the mountain of myrrh.[2] Do not banish me, do not cast me out from the land of the living. My garment is blackened, my shoes are torn. Take me on your shoulders, Volmar, carry me northward.

Hildegard sits up; her neck and back are stiff. She tastes death, licks the taste of death from her lips, pulls Volmar's hood farther over his face, draws the sleeves of his habit over his hands. We had a good time, and we knew it, but you couldn't bring Richardis back to me, you could not take the pain about Richardis from me. How long ago that is, more than twenty years, you had read the letters out loud, letters

[2] See Song of Songs 4:6; and cf. *Scivias* III. 13. 16; Letter to Abbot Helenger (Letter 15 in Fox, ed., *Book of Divine Works,* 303).

of complaint from the monasteries, and then there was one more letter, and when you began to read it, you grew pale: they wanted Richardis of Stade to be abbess of Birsim.

Hildegard threw up her hands before her face: no, not that, not that again, not now. I am tired, Volmar, tired and old. There is no flight to the mountain of myrrh. Don't leave me alone. Just now we were sitting in the midday sun, my hand lay on your knee, your strength pushed me up, just now you handed me the bowl. If we had not walked out at high noon, you would have been resting. Then the bell calls to Matins and Lauds. Do not banish me as a stranger from the land of the living. I am a pilgrim in the shadow of death. Do not cut off the light from the light. We had a good time. Good-bye. We are heroes. She kisses his mouth. *Lux perpetua, lux perpetua. Transire ad vitam. De morte transire ad vitam.*[3] I should concern myself with the sisters, thinks Hildegard, they look tired and worn out with weeping. *De morte ad vitam transire.*

But why were the oxen lying in the fruit orchard? Hildegard felt her way forward, a stick in either hand in order not to have to walk alone. For four weeks she had lain stiff, combed through and through by pain, but now she had defied orders and begun to walk again. The midday rest is a good time, the attendant is sleeping, deeply asleep after all her weeks of watching. Hildegard stumbles; the sticks are always wanting to go differently than her legs, her feet are always in the way. And now there are the oxen lying in the fruit orchard. But when she sees Gimbert in the apple tree, she knows for certain: he has to do two things at once. The animals are well behaved, lying under the apple tree, chewing their cuds, peacefully as if they were fed heavenly food. She puts aside her sticks. I think I can walk alone, I have two feet, it is true they have no toes, but I have two legs, it is true they have no joints, but they are better than sticks.

Hello, Hildegard, catch: here is the most beautiful apple,

[3] Perpetual light, perpetual light. To go into life. To go from death into life.

catch it. And Hildegard makes a great bowl of her skirt. Throw it gently, Gimbert, throw it as if you were tossing the universe into my lap. Look out, Hildegard, this is no universe, but it is the most magnificent apple on this tree. And Gimbert throws gently; how strong the spread skirt in the little hands already is! The apple is wonderfully beautiful. Throw the others into my skirt, too, I will catch them and put them into the basket, they will not even feel the change from branch to nest. And Gimbert plucks, throws, aiming at Hildegard's dress, takes his time, throws again. And the child laughs, and all her joints are healed. When the tree is empty, I will catch you; my dress is very strong, all my limbs are alive again.

And Hildegard catches and grabs and catches and lays in the basket, and Gimbert is no longer in any hurry at all, and when he has to climb higher in the tree, Hildegard swiftly kisses Romulus's ear and whispers: pretty soon Gimbert will jump, right into my dress, and she rejoices in the oxen's agreement. The animals nod, chew, grass grows rampant around their flanks. Wait a moment, Gimbert, there is so much to see here, let me look at the blooming grass around the hips of the animals, it is blooming in tiny umbels, and their hips are shimmering. When you come down, you will see.

But Gimbert calls: look out, catch, we are not finished yet. You have to practice catching, you can't practice enough. One must be able to catch. Dear Gimbert. And then he jumps, of course not into Hildegard's dress, but so that he touches her dress and she falls down. And there they both lie, laughing, and Gimbert lifts Hildegard high and holds her up in the air, so that she swings back and forth, a feather, and a current bears her up so that she may not sink, and the oxen chew the blooming grass. Come, we will carry the baskets into the house. And Gimbert carries all the weight.

Requiem aeternam et lux perpetua. Beati mortui. Amodo jam ut requiescat a laboribus. Et lux perpetua luceat ei.[4] How clear and strong

---

[4] Eternal rest and perpetual light. Blessed are the dead. May he henceforth rest from his labors. And may perpetual light shine upon him.

was Mechthild's voice. Do not cast the eye from the eye, do not cut off the light from the light.

Later, a delegation came from St. Disibod to collect Volmar's body. Hugo also came: you need a new secretary, the work must not be cut off. I have two well-schooled scribes, said Hildegard, and I can govern the monastery myself. You need a provost, and you need a man who is in command of his Latin. Yes, yes, said Hildegard. The men spoke of a monk named Gottfried. No rabbit, no lark, a declining summer. I am Volmar, you can tell me if you have any problems, we will imagine the grill away. And our *lingua ignota*?[5] Your big ear. Yes, yes, said Hildegard, send Gottfried or someone else, he must have good Latin. And when the men had refreshed themselves they came out with a sack in which they had placed Volmar's body, and they loaded the sack onto a horse and rode away. And Hildegard stood in the gate with the key in her hand and looked after the baggage train. Dear God!

Then she locked the gate and went through Volmar's entrance into the scriptorium, saw his table, the chair with its crumpled rug, saw the pens, penknife, pumice stones, and on the last page three lines of very beautiful, clear writing. She felt the sharp bite of her teeth in her knuckles. Finally she pulled the curtain across the window, packed everything together and carried it outside and back around into her scriptorium. Read to me what Volmar last wrote, she said. And Hiltrud read: There is a certain serpent, a very hot one, that. No, said Hildegard, it should read:

> There is a certain very hot serpent that can live in water and on land and that devises devilish spite and snares against human beings. For this kind of serpent is the enemy of humanity, blows out its breath against them and is full of deadly poison. [Write, said Hildegard] If a person kills it and carefully takes out its heart, dries it in the sun and preserves it and, when oppressed by great sorrow and pain, takes it in

---

[5] Unknown language.

194

the right hand, that person will not only be joyful but is also secure against all poison as long as it is held in the hand.[6]

It went very slowly. Again and again Hiltrud had to search laboriously for words, look them up, and then she was not sure of the case or the construction. Leave it, said Hildegard finally, the worm is not all that important. Or wait, put this down in German:

> The tree-frog is more warm than cold and grows from the air that the trees produce from their leaves and flowers. When they are producing it, the spirits offer more temptations to human beings than at other times, since then the human sense is more attuned to the vanities of play and laughter. At such times people also, through devilish spite, practice idolatry and all sorts of vanities with this snake. If one wishes to prevent the devil's arts from being practiced on him or her, it is necessary to throw a tree-frog into a bath of mercury. It is of absolutely no use as a medicine.[7]

"Mercury bath," it must read, she said. Hiltrud sighed, and rubbed out the whole line with the pumice stone. We can go into the chapel, said Hildegard, the bell will be ringing for Vespers shortly.

[6] *Naturkunde*, 139.
[7] Ibid., 95–96.

Pilgrim in the Shadow of Death

Disturbance at the gate, shouts, calls for Hildegard; she still has the key in her hand. A man covered with blood is roaring like a bull; he collapses. Cloths, water. Hildegard kneels, wipes the blood from his face: both his eyes have been gouged out, both eyes. Water, cloths. Help me, Clementia!

When the bleeding has stopped, Hildegard washes the man's face and hands, binds a cloth about his eyes, covers him with a blanket, lays another in her lap and nestles his head in it.

You can't sit there like that, says Mechthild, we will carry him into the sick room. No, don't move him, says Hildegard; get some hot wine. Drop after drop she pours on the corners of his mouth, then through his nose. That loosens the man's teeth from his tongue, and he drinks. Who did this, asks Hildegard, who? But the stranger does not answer; he turns his head aside and sleeps. Hildegard sits there, crosslegged, the sleeping man's head in her lap, stroking his forehead, one of his hands, the calluses, the torn nails. I am like ashes and blowing dust. A pilgrim in the shadow of death.

Then she hums softly to herself. Our backs are a street for wanderers. The gate is still open; she sits between its angles with the stranger in her lap, nailed fast, riveted, hammered down, sees yesterday's path losing itself in the field, sees the sky from which the light is fading, not a lark, not a rabbit, Volmar is sitting on the stone, a horse is harnessed to it and pulls the stone away, another horse jumps ahead, Richardis's back is straight, she turns her head, her brows flash, mirror of the moon's path: I will become abbess of Birsim, my brother wishes it, my mother wishes it, and so do I, the weather is clear, the roads are dry, in three days I will be in Birsim.

The moon's paths flash, her coif is straight as a string and blindingly white. I must go after her, I will strike Heinrich of Mainz and the marchioness and Hartwig of Bremen on the chest with my fists. Abbess, that child! The north with its dark sky, the contrary winds, the salty air. Come back. One must not undertake that to which one is not equal.

> Oh shepherds, weep and wail in this time, for you know not what you are doing when you throw away the offices of God's foundation for the sake of money and for the foolishness of bad people who do not fear God. Protect yourselves from the destruction of your souls.[8]

[8] *Briefwechsel,* 95–96.

She goes to Volmar's window: it must not be that the child should go this way, I must protect her. She presses forward in the furrow, with screaming arms against the north wind that strikes her face; I will bring you back, you will walk on the moon's path. Then she feels the hand on her shoulder. She is dead, Hildegard, says Volmar. Take back your anger. Close up your longing.

Come, sister, that is enough. The stranger is well. Arnulf will lead him. The night presses black through the gate. A thousand years are for you like yesterday, already past. Come, sister, we will bring you to your bed.

Hildegard's illness lasted sixty days. Carved in stone. Change of attendants night and day. Eye torn from eye, light cut off from light. Shadow of death. Song and prayer scarcely audible, the bells thin. The sick silent. The trees stiffen, the waters freeze. Snow covers the Rupertsberg. The sky is swollen with darkness. Light cut off from light. Carved in stone. Washings with wine vinegar. Mechthild at the prie-dieu, Wineldis at the stove, Gottfried in the scriptorium. The spindle, the needle, the weaver's reed, the powder, the ointments. The snow piles up around the monastery. Sometimes Berengar gropes his way under Hildegard's window and hums a song. Hugo looks after the sisters, comforts the women. Sometimes at night, when she is sure that no one else is coming, Walburgis takes off her coif and wraps Hildegard's body in her hair. Carved in stone. Eye torn from eye. Christmas. The new year. Burn out the wounds with torches.

Then a crane circles over the monastery. Awake and stir yourself, I have taken from your hand the cup of staggering; you shall drink no more from the bowl of my wrath. Your children have fainted, they lie at the head of every street. Your tormentors have said to you, "Bow down, that we may walk on you," and you have made your back like the ground and like the street for them to walk on.[9]

[9] Isaiah 51:20-23.

197

Hildegard sat up; her hands and elbows were without skin; she breathes. Hiltrud holds her head, Clementia braces her back. Forgive me, says Hildegard, forgive me.

Vere dignum et justum est. [10] The bells rang the recovery. The sisters sang and wept.

[10] It is truly meet and just.

Rescue from the Horns of the Buffalo

There are fish that, by their nature, live on the floor of the seas and rivers. They seek their food there, rummaging in the mud. They eat the roots of certain plants, and from these they live a long time. They also find many other things that appeal to them as nourishment. At times they ascend to a higher level of the waters, but they soon return to the bottom, where they remain most of the time. Their flesh is somewhat soft and without strength and is not healthful because they always live at the bottom of the waters. Some of them prefer the day and the light of the sun to the night and the light of the moon, others the reverse. Other fish live primarily at a medium depth in clear water and seek their food there. Sometimes they find plants on overhanging rocks that are so healthful that if human beings could find these plants they could use them to eliminate all sickness. Since they eat these plants and live in pure water, these fish have strong flesh and are nourishing. Sometimes they swim to the bottom, but soon rise again and remain for the most part in the middle depth of the waters. They are somewhat smaller than the fish that ordinarily live at the bottom. Of these also, some prefer the day and the sunlight, others the night and the moonlight. The same grouping is also found among fish that live at the surface of the seas and rivers and seek their food in the foam and the considerable filth that floats there. They are penetrated by the sun more than the fish that live deeper. Since thcy conceal themselves in certain coves with foul, stinking water their flesh is soft, without strength, and unhealthful.[11]

Hildegard spoke slowly, evenly, and Gottfried sat deeply bowed beneath his enormous hood and wrote what Hildegard dictated, not questioning, never requesting a pause, not correcting, only writing. There was no struggling together over a word, a grammatical question, a stylistic figure. This was a man in command of Latin.

> The crab is more warm than cold and derives its warmth more from the earth than from the air. It loves both night and day, because it goes forward like the sun and backward like the moon. It has healthful flesh. Its head contains something fresh, called "crebeszmar." If it is mixed with butter it produces a smooth skin without pimples.[12]

In writing letters, too, Gottfried indicated no interest when Hildegard warned against the paths of the many, the wages of death, complained about the effeminate age, recommended to the rich that they reject dangling earrings and not decline the discipline of the hair shirt, warned that the hen that crows in thc night brings terror on itself. He wrote it all down silently, letter after letter. And Hildegard had no desire to push his hood back. She sat with her hands in her lap, making her words into sounds. "There is a certain fish that is covered with mussels. It is not edible. It loves the night, lives on the bottom and feeds on unclean things."[13]

To go to the river at midday and look at the fish. I can catch fish, shall I catch them for you, I have a fishing-net and a landing-net, look, I can dive, too, I will get you an eel, it washes itself in pure water and fertilizes the weeds on the river-bank. "It fears storms and the great waves that then arise,

---

[11] *Naturkunde,* 91–92.
[12] Ibid., 100.
[13] Ibid., 98.

so much so that when it hears thunder it presses itself into such small holes that it cannot get out of them again, and so dies. Its liver can give strength to your heart.''[14] Look how I can dive with the net. Hildegard sees two brown feet disappearing in the water, and then the young face, the eyes feathered with brown and blue and the moon-path eyebrows washed with water, glistening in the light, and she has to weep. And the boy with Richardis's face throws the fish back into the water.

Come, Hildegard, the bell has rung for Vespers.

Hildegard's strength increased daily. She stood at the oven and approved the bread; she stood at the stove and tasted the soup. She was in the weaving room and measured the woolen socks, sniffed the apples in the cellar, tasted the wine, stirred the pastes in the ointment kitchen, placed the warming blankets on the benches in the chapel. Create breadth for me in my narrowness. You have put gladness in my heart more than when their grain and wine abound. How very good and pleasant it is when kindred live together in unity! It is like the dew of Hermon, which falls on the mountains of Zion. For there the Lord ordained a blessing, life forever.[15]

Ordained is a lovely word, she thought. Go out in the snow, she said to the sisters, and rub your faces clean, we are not prisoners. I will write a song cycle and you will perform it; hunt out the white veils and see if the moths have eaten them, and let your hair grow again. Listen to the song about St. Rupert, and she sang, softly and clear, *et O tu, Ruperte, qui es socius eorum in hac habitatione, succurrite nobis famulantibus et in exilio laborantibus.*[16] Happiness at Rupertsberg.

The poultry squawked, the swine grunted contentedly, the sheep bleated. We will have a rich crop of wool in the spring,

[14] Ibid., 97.

[15] Psalm 4:7; 133:1, 3.

[16] And O Rupert, you who are their companion in this dwelling, help us, serving and laboring in exile. *Symphonia* V. 49. 10.

said Berengar, and many lambs, too. You have everything in order, Berengar, and it is clean here. Don't send me away. No, said Hildegard, I won't send you away. I don't need my eyes when I am here. Hildegard stroked his cheek. I like your singing; sing a little. Hildegard sat down, took a sheep in her arms, and listened. Let me ride on it once, Gimbert, just once. She hitched up her skirt, and Gimbert grabbed her under the arms, lifted her high and set her on the sheep. I don't weigh anything, Gimbert, and in a minute it will jump into the air with me on it, and fly away, and I am not afraid. The sheep's coat whispered in her hands. But then Gimbert took her down and said they were not made for riding, and no one can fly with them, not even you. No, said Hildegard, they were not made for riding, you are right, but their wool whispers and smells of I don't know what. Give me your cloak, she said to Berengar, I want to go out and see how far away the light is. And Berengar brought his cloak, laid it on Hildegard's shoulders, pulled stockings over her sandals. The paths are slippery, the stockings will keep you from falling. There sat Hildegard in the shepherd's cloak that bowed her shoulders, and felt Berengar's tenderness as he pulled the stockings over her sandals. Flying sheep and lambs.

Icy air struck Hildegard, gray whiteness on the paths, the bushes and the trees. A pair of doves in the linden tree, only a shade grayer than the sky. It is not the time for love's caresses. But soon the light will grow stronger, the water in the springs will thaw. Berengar told her of the black goats in his homeland, the dangers in the mountains, the seeking and finding. Hildegard held him by the hand. It is always time for love's caresses, she thought, and gave him back his cloak and stockings. You must let me know when the lambs come, she called again.

But when she wanted to think out her song cycle during the siesta, she fell asleep. She sits on a throne, clothed in a cloak of birds' feathers and a crown of birds' eyes. A cat lies beside her clawed feet. She devours her children, soldiers with red, snoutlike mouths drag in a woman with an iron ring about her neck. She devours her children, they shout, she bears them, fattens them, slaughters and cooks them, devours them with pleasure, only their hearts does she bury in the forests. Seventeen times she has borne, seventeen times slaughtered and eaten, seventeen hearts are turning to stone in the forest. They pull so hard on the chain that the head is cut off by the neck ring and flies into Hildegard's lap. The cat sits up, hisses, bares its teeth, lashes its tail. No, cries Hildegard, no, and pulls the cloak around the head, no, and wakes.

Alas, the walls of my heart. One should not sleep at midday, I must break this habit. She shook herself, rubbed her face, hands and arms. My skin is much too big for me. Criseldis, ring for None. But there is no ringing. The head, the cat, the crown of birds' eyes. If my tabernacle desires to accomplish the works of injustice, I will tread down marrow, blood and flesh with patience and defend myself like a strong lion. And if rage lowers around my tent, I will be softer than the air that, with its light waftings, moistens the dryness of the earth. I will not turn aside from the fragile earth, but contend valiantly against it. But my skin is much too big. St. Benedict!

Quail Arise from the Sea for Refreshment

Gottfried was reading a letter. Read it again, said Hildegard. "Your fruitfulness is better for us than wine and sweeter-smelling than the most precious ointments." What long sentences, thought Hildegard, and what imagery.

> You draw us after you. Since, therefore, my lady, I cannot personally see your face, which, as I believe, reflects the divine light, let me at least hear your voice by letter. For your voice is dear to me. And that I may not only have you in mind

like the image reflected by a mirror, may the image of your sanctity enlighten me and dwell within the thoughts of my heart the more often and the more deeply.[17]

Thoughts of the heart. She had not heard everything, but she needed no repetition. Who is this Wibert of Gembloux? Gottfried did not know. Hildegard wanted to answer Wibert's letter, but she did not know what she should write, and she grew evasive when Gottfried pressed her. I am sinking in deep mud, my wounds are rotten and oozing because of my foolishness. The words ran after her. Where is Gembloux? A visitor drew it on a map: a broad river, an arrow pointing northwest, a smaller river with a bend: Gembloux lies within that bend. How far is it as a bird flies, how long does a snail need to go there, how many stones would make a road to it? A thousand, thousand years. Two blackbirds in the branches of the maple tree. Two gypsies at a charcoal fire. You draw us after you. Hildegard tried to forget the letter.

Then a second letter came with the same plea. "The cleverest masters make a great outcry from dry hearts and puffed-out cheeks, but you slake the thirst of the thirsty!"[18] His intention toward me is love, thought Hildegard and dictated, wondering at the length and the frankness of her description of her visions.

> But I am constantly filled with fear and trembling, for I recognize no security in myself through any kind of personal ability. Still I lift up my hands to God that I may be held by God, just like a feather that, with no weight of its own strength, allows itself to be blown about by the wind. But as long as I see it, all sorrow and anxiety is taken from me, so that I feel myself to be like a simple young girl and not like an old woman. . . . But you also: take heed of the eagle who flies toward the clouds with its two wings. If it lost its wings, it would fall to earth and not be able to raise itself again, no matter how much it wishes to lift itself in flight. So also the

[17] *Briefwechsel*, 224–25; cf. Song of Songs 1:3-4.
[18] *Briefwechsel*, 226.

human being flies with the two wings of reason, namely the knowledge of good (the right wing) and the knowledge of evil (the left wing). The knowledge of evil serves the good, for the good is made keener and guided by the knowledge of evil, and so through this knowledge the human being becomes wise in all things. . . . In the zeal of your desire for heaven you have kept your eyes on the mountain peak, beyond all the crags and clefts.[19]

What on earth is she talking about! Gottfried wrote dumbly, corrected nothing, but his eyes were curious. Who is Wibert of Gembloux? Volmar would have said: we will cut out this, and this; restrain yourself. Volmar. What would he have thought of Wibert's letters? A dreamer. A fiery Walloon. She closed her eyes, but she could not hear Volmar's voice, could not catch its sound. No hare. No lark. A declining summer. Time lived out. Hildegard tried to remove Wibert of Gembloux from the thoughts of her heart.

The sick people, scratched, bitten by vermin, exhausted by work, martyred by sorrow. Truly, the hills are a delusion, the orgies on the mountains. Let us lie down in our shame, and let our dishonor cover us.[20] It is terrible to be born.

And high summer, the rampant growth of the grasses, the red and black berries bulging, the cherries beginning to gleam, the quinces, grass blooming around the flanks of the lambs, soon to be full-grown sheep, the roses exploding with joy. It is good to be born. A row of tall trees on the right, a row of tall trees on the left, their crowns interlacing. The leaves become words, whispering and muttering, rolling themselves out and in, becoming red and brown. Cut the leaves from the tree for me. But Wibert, Wibert of Gembloux laughs. He blows a powerful breath; there is buzzing and cooing. Like an advancing shadow I go in, like a grasshopper I will be

[19] Ibid., 226–28; see Fox, ed., *Book of Divine Works,* Letter 39, to Wibert of Gembloux, 348–51.
[20] Jeremiah 3:23, 25.

shaken off. Then Wibert takes his sword and cuts a path into the crowns. And sky breaks through. Take heed of the eagle who flies toward the clouds; if it loses its wings it falls to earth. Clefts in the crags, desire for heaven. Take heed how you fly.

A messenger arrives: Wibert of Gembloux is on his way. Oh my goodness, cried Hildegard, and ran to the kitchen to speak with Wineldis about the entertainment of the guest. Not finding the sister, she ran into the garden to see about the roses, the pumpkin, it is dry and cold, feeds on the air, is good for the healthy as well as for the sick. Cut in slices and marinated in honey with spices. Hildegard bent down: it is like skin in which miracles are waiting. She stood up, puffing, went to the well, sat down and drew her name in her secret writing on the surface of the water, and Volmar's name as well. I will rest here in the sun for a moment, warm my knees and hand.

The pumpkin grew, four bearers came, lifted it onto a sled and dragged it away. Stop, called Hildegard, and ran after them on winged feet; we must slaughter it; the pumpkin grew still bigger, and more and more bearers came running, the wings on her feet caught fire, the flames drove them back. Hildegard rubbed her neck and stood up; her legs had gone to sleep and she had to hold on to the well to keep from falling. I am getting old, I am always dozing off. I am an old woman with blazing, fiery wings on feet that have fallen asleep.

The next day, Wibert of Gembloux and his party were standing at the gate. The autumn wind was blowing his habit. His curls are like the panicles of dates, black as ravens. His eyes are like doves at the streams of water. Hildegard gave the men the cup of welcome and Gottfried helped her when she did not understand everything that Wibert was saying about the journey. An arched mouth, a nicely-curved nose, curls as black as ravens. Then they made a tour of the monastery, and Wibert admired the fire in the kitchen, the bakery, the workshops, the barns with the poultry and sheep; he greeted the sisters, praised the good order, and Hildegard showed him the herb garden, the orchard, the autumn roses, stood with him at the well and said: write your name in the water, and Wibert did as she asked, writing deeply and with large letters. Living water. Eyes like doves at the streams, bathed in milk. The bell rang for Sext and they all went into the chapel. Hildegard heard how Wibert pronounced "angelus" with a soft "g," and it added a new sound alongside their hard "g." Lovely, thought Hildegard, very lovely that life is not yet ended. It is good, Wibert of Gembloux, that you have come.

The meal passed in silence. Wibert rolled the wine on his tongue a little while before swallowing it, ate slowly and listened to the reading. His arms are rounded gold, set with jewels from Tarshish.[21] After None we will meet in the scriptorium.

Hildegard lay on her bed, laid her arms down also, with open hands. Lie like this, just lie like this. She saw Wibert's hands, his mouth, his eyes, and she wept, wept from within herself and into herself and knew not why. Draw me after you. That I may not only keep you in mind like the image reflected in a mirror. May your image dwell within the thoughts of my heart. In the zeal of your desire for heaven you have kept your eyes on the mountain peak, beyond all the crags and clefts.

At None, Wibert was not in the chapel. He was sitting in the scriptorium with Gottfried. They were discussing legal matters, documents, letters of protection, gifts, St. Disibod, names she had never heard. That much she understood. Her saliva tasted like brick dust. His arms are rounded gold, set with jewels from Tarshish. It was about her, the preservation of her person for the world to come. She left the scriptorium. We two, she said to Berengar, will wash the sheep's ears now, at last I have time. Sloe juice in warm water, sponges found between the rocks. Berengar held the sheep, sang, and Hildegard soaked the sponge, washed out the ears of one sheep

[21] Cf. Song of Songs 5:14.

after another, and their eyes at the same time. The animals loved it, even when Hildegard pulled the filth out of their ears with her little finger. Feel how soft the skin is inside their ears, and how finely the interior of their ears is made. She guided Berengar's finger, thought of Jutta, of Volmar, and her heart was sore. Enough of visitors and disturbance. Now their ears and eyes are shining, she said. But Wibert did not appear at Vespers, either. What kind of order did they keep in Gembloux, then?

Wibert had plucked a bouquet of grasses, branches with nuts on them, berries and baskets of fruit, reddish beech leaves. Beauty, fruitfulness, decay. She takes the bouquet from his hands. Long are the broad ways of the world that lead to death. Forecourts of heaven. I will set his hand on the sea and his right hand on the rivers. My faithfulness and steadfast love will be with him.[22]

After Compline they went back to the refectory again. You have been in my house a whole day and I have scarcely seen you. I washed the sheep's ears instead of going out into the autumn with you. Before the mountains were born—you know what I mean. And Hildegard began to tell him the things she had already written in her letter. Gottfried had nodded off; the sisters withdrew one after the other. She told him of her brothers and sisters, her father and the stars, Gimbert and Romulus, the swing and the pine trees that are an image of strength, er-high, er-high, of her fear of swinging over the top.

And Wibert listened, helped her now and then with a word or part of a phrase. The last pinewood spill went out; they crept into the kitchen and sat before the fire. The heat sent up a flame, and Wibert put on another log. Hildegard told him about the angels and the stones, the sardonyx that frees people from anger, foolishness and lust, and the dill, the sun and the crane, the moon and the lynx and the ride in the boat. St. Disibod, Jutta, the great altar cloth, the birds when Jutta died, the building, Robert, the well. One must always begin

[22] Psalm 89:24-25.

with the well and take care that the sun strikes into it so that the water will not go bad. Volmar. That was a long, good time. Hiltrud. Rupert. Sickness and Rupertsberg. The fields. The sick. The king brought me to the banquet house, his intention toward me was love. Sustain me with raisins, refresh me with apples, for I am faint with love.[23]

And Wibert answered: draw me after you. We will exult and rejoice in you, we will extol your love more than wine; rightly do they love you.[24] And then they began to take the bouquet apart, ate the blackberries, shelled the nuts, threw the shells into the fire, ate the kernels, the elderberries, spat the holly drops into the heat. Two gypsies on the path toward the forecourts of heaven. Two blackbirds in the branches of the maple tree. Awake, O north wind, and come, O south wind! Blow upon my garden that its fragrance may be wafted abroad. Let my beloved come to his garden and eat its choicest fruits. Come, my beloved, let us go forth into the fields, and lodge in the villages; let us go out early to the vineyards, and see whether the vines have budded, whether the grape blossoms have opened, and the pomegranates are in bloom.[25] Good night.

If I could, I would wash the lions' ears tomorrow. His arms are rounded gold, set with jewels from Tarshish. Many waters cannot quench love, neither can floods drown it. If one offered for love all the wealth of his house, it would be utterly scorned.[26] I cry out with joy to the Lord and I am secure. Just look at the fullness; the grape contains a fiery heat, it shines in the sun like rubies. Before the flood, the earth was fragile and bore no wine, but now, having been strengthened by the flood, it brings forth wine. We must roll the stone aside, come, I will draw you after me, we will go all the way in and see the darkness that lets us hear our hearts. Don't be afraid,

---

[23] Song of Songs 2:4-5.
[24] Song of Songs 1:4.
[25] Song of Songs 4:16; 7:11-12.
[26] Song of Songs 5:14; 8:7; cf. Psalm 35:9.

come with winged steps. And there the light appears, with a bluish shimmer. That is how I know that you love me, that my enemy cannot rejoice over me. They take one another's hands, leave the vineyard, roll the stone over the entrance. If you have a contract with the stones of the field, you must keep it. Beautiful beloved. My hands drip with liquid myrrh upon the handles of the bolt.[27] Now go back to Gembloux and come again before I die, long before I die, come back again.

[27] Song of Songs 5:5.

O these
armies of the day,
that want to trip us up.
We will
arm ourselves well
with the lances
of love.

XVII

Wolves Cannot Swallow the Sun

Hildegard had again forbidden herself to sleep during the siesta, and since Gottfried desperately needed his midday rest, she was free. She preferred to go into the garden, tie up a plant, weed a part of a bed, set out a cutting, rake a path. She opened her ears to the birds' singing and extinguished the burning of her eyes in the greenness. When she found a stone she washed it in the well, watched it as it dried, breathed on it and rubbed it smooth on her sleeve and laid it together with the others. Nothing but pebbles. But they are fallen angels like the other stones, and all of them are effective against melancholy and sadness, quarrelsomeness and violent temper, sleepwalking and delusions. Nothing but fallen angels, the pebbles too. If I did not have to be me, I would be a stone that makes the eyes clear.

Sister, you are dreaming. Hugo was standing before her. You must do something for your bones, said Hildegard, you are getting shorter. Drutwin is dead, said Hugo. I wanted to bring you the news myself. So, Drutwin. Did they bury him at Bermersheim? Hugo nodded. He was a big eater, said Hildegard, and a great hunter. Father was very fond of him. He managed the estate wisely, said Hugo; he increased the inheritance and turned the servants into leaseholders. His son, our nephew was here once, said Hildegard, but I can't recall his face. Drutwin, then. May God receive his soul in friendship.

Hugo put his arm around his sister and led her into the house. I bring greetings from Adelheid. She is a clever abbess. She knows the rules, said Hildegard, she is in command of her body and her feelings, she understands how to combine strictness with gentleness. She is lonesome for you, said Hugo. Yes, yes. She is my dear child and always will be. I never had any trouble with her. She can pray without hesitating, and she drinks water as if it were wine. One day I was telling her about Simon Peter and Thomas and the others who were coming back weary and without any fish, and about the one who had kindled a fire on shore and prepared fish and bread and said: come and eat. You forgot, she interrupted, that he first sent the men back, even though they were tired, and only waited on them when they brought their full net to shore.[1] She was right, she is one of those who have healthy souls. And Richardis? To be on the shore, conscious of hunger and weariness, kindling a fire: come and eat. Full nets here, full nets there. I will write to Adelheid. Drutwin, then.

And then, in the middle of the winter, Gottfried. Had Hildegard seen nothing but the enormous hood, not his blue lips, his pale nose, had she heard nothing but those words? He lay there groaning, the corners of his mouth turned down, his left arm beside him. Tea, drops, ointment, moist cloths; Hildegard placed one hand on the other and assisted the weak pumping of his heart until her coif was wet. Why don't I let him die? But she did not let him die, she applied all her arts and all her strength to keep his heart going. For three weeks. She saw him dying, saw him expiring, stopped pumping, stroked his arm, sang the prayers. The suffering disappeared, little by little, from his face, and was replaced by a smile. *Beati mortui, qui in Domino moriuntur. Ego sum panis vivus, requiescat a laboribus.*[2]

Hildegard was surprised that she was not sad. She gave the body over to Arnulf, went into the kitchen, held her hands over the warm ashes, went out into the snow, ate a handful, rubbed her face with it. *Transire ad vitam.*[3] She laid herself on her bed and waited for the fur to warm her.

The earth was frozen hard. Two farmers stood with their legs wide apart and swung their pickaxes with both hands, over their heads and down into the earth that only gave way

[1] John 21.

[2] Blessed are the dead who die in the Lord. I am the living bread, may he rest from his labors.

[3] To pass over into life.

one clod at a time and with a hollow ring. You must dig deep, said Hildegard, deeper than usual, down to where the earth is soft and warm. You must crush the clods; we can't throw those big chunks on him. When the grave is finished, you must cover it with straw. Perhaps we could also put a pot full of coals inside, she thought, and shuddered with cold. I should help them, then I would be warm, but she only listened to the toneless sound and echo that the picks wrung from the earth.

When she began to be afraid that her feet would freeze fast to the earth she went into the house, went to the kitchen to order hot beer for the farmers, and discussed the ceremonies with Mechthild. She went back into the kitchen and talked with Wineldis and Alfriede about the hospitality to be given on the day of burial; mourners would come from St. Disibod. She went into the herb kitchen. An herb against death. Benedict's herb, she said to Clementia, is an aphrodisiac. The sick have confirmed that for me; it is good for bringing back the declining powers of the body, and—she saw the sister's closed face—besides that, the cool leaves of the plantain have proved very effective for burns and glandular swellings, you were right, we should be able to preserve them, the tinctures are not nearly so effective. You have sometimes been surly of late, said Hildegard softly. Clementia kept on working. You would have done better to leave Walburgis with the chickens and ducks instead of sending her to me in the ointment kitchen, she murmured.

Hildegard was relieved. If that is all, you have no need to be jealous, we need successors and Walburgis has healing hands. Then Clementia began to weep. Hildegard drew her close to her on the bench. When had she ever seen the sisters weeping? She laid her hands on Clementia's hands, waited silently, feeling her dry skin, the gouty deposits. She is old. We are old. There was only a dry sobbing like that of someone who has forgotten how to weep. Clementia stood up and went back to her stirring. Hildegard sat there with empty hands and looked at the growing hump on her sister's back. She would have liked to put her arms around her, but she did not; she went out. There will be no flight to the mountain of myrrh.

And there lay Gottfried, his hands folded within the sleeves of his habit, his face gray and lightless, the suggestion of a smile erased. Hildegard sat down on the altar steps, embraced her knees, rested her chin on her thumbs. *Resuscitabo in novissimo die, in novissimo die resuscitabo.*[4] Frozen earth, toneless thuds. It may be that the sky is full of new snow. Perhaps even the day after tomorrow the air will smell of spring. The sisters came in for Sext. Hildegard took her place.

I need a new provost, said Hildegard, when she sat with Hugo and the abbot of St. Disibod in the scriptorium after the ceremonies. The sisterhood is growing. I need a new scribe, my work is not complete, I don't have much more time. Gottfried has written my vita, but who is going to check it? Was Gottfried an appropriate man? asked the abbot. He did his duty, was diligent and a little bit naive about miracles. He was the kind of person for whom you have to warm up the grave. Wibert of Gembloux would be the right person, said the abbot; I will see about it. Wibert of Gembloux, thought Hildegard. Catch us the foxes, the little foxes that ruin the vineyards, for our vineyards are in blossom.[5] Until then, said the abbot, Hugo will remain here. She looked at her brother. All the sparkle has gone out of him, only the ring on his finger still shines. No, no, no, the paths are not ready for the flight to the mountain of myrrh. But the wolves cannot devour the sun.[6]

---

[4] I will raise them up on the last day, on the last day I will raise them up.
[5] Song of Songs 2:15.
[6] Cf. *Scivias* III. 11. 6-7; *De operatione Dei* III. 10. 34.

215

Only One Direction for Heaven and Earth

Hildegard wandered past Gottfried's grave: dahlias in bunches, purple brown, threads of light, lovely, lovely. Flower petals like thick silk, fullness itself. How often has the earth, formerly crushed, been softened, what was formerly frozen been warmed. Formerly! Hildegard sat down on the curb of the well, names written in water, veilings of the sky, foliage ready to be cast off, the summer's sequel, a thrush with open beak, feathers spread to drink in the sunshine. Come soon, Wibert of Gembloux. She stretched, her joints creaking, her toes curling like horns. Walburgis's hair around my knees. But Walburgis was in Eibingen, had been for a long time now, her hair shorn before she left. Hildegard sighed.

Is there anyone in the world who lacks the knowledge of good and evil?

> Together with the knowledge of good and evil, human beings possess the love of God and the fear of God. Having these two abilities, they should take the plow in hand and make their fields fruitful. They should shun and eradicate all weeds, and they must not be negligent in this work. This is a majestic testimony and a great matter, for heaven and earth are not able to overturn the law that governs them, since heaven and earth can take no other direction than the one appointed for them. But those who know the desire for life, let them take up these words and hold them fast within, in the chamber of their hearts.[7]

Take the plow in hand. A majestic testimony. A great matter, only one direction for heaven and earth. Bound together by light.

I heard you speaking, said Berengar. I wanted to show you the sheep. They have been pasturing under apple trees; their wool is like silk. And are their ears clean? I sometimes sing

---

[7] *LVM,* 118.

songs in their ears, said Berengar; that cleans them. Yes, yes, thought Hildegard, washing the ears with songs, that is something one must be able to do. Do you want to tell me anything? asked Berengar softly. You know that about the multiplication of the loaves, don't you, the five thousand men, the twelve baskets. Berengar nodded. Jesus wanted to be alone, so the disciples had to go ahead of him in the boat. But when he saw that the boat was being tossed about by the winds, he came down from the mountain and walked over the water toward the boat. The disciples were beside themselves with fear. Fear not. If it is you, called Peter, tell me to come to you across the water, and Jesus said, come. Peter got out of the boat and walked on the water, but the strong wind made him afraid, and he began to sink and called for help. Then Jesus stretched out his hand, took Peter's hand and said softly, oh you of little faith, why did you doubt. And Peter was ashamed, but at the same time he was very glad to hold the other's hand. And so they both got into the boat, and the wind was calm. And they all knew of it and were very happy.[8]

So, if one is afraid, one will sink? Yes, said Hildegard, thinking of Jutta and of Hiltrud's disgust. But a hand keeps one from sinking if one is without courage. You should see it, Berengar, my toes were dusty with the summer earth, and the sheep has licked them clean. Then Berengar went away on light feet as if he were walking on water, like a visionary. To walk on water and escape the enemy, thought Hildegard. She turned her face to the sun and closed her eyes. The creation of heaven and earth, of day and night and the foundation of consciousness; the creation of the firmament, the water, the fixed land, the heaven, and discernment, so that good and evil are distinguishable; the creation of earth and seas, plants, trees and the measure of our way of living; the creation of sun, moon and stars and the love of God and neighbor; the creation of fish and fowl and the building up of the life of grace; the creation of snakes, wild beasts, human beings and the

[8] Matthew 14.

growth of the life of virtue: six days of creation and then, with the day of rest, the perfection of the virtues.

She sighed and stood up; it would ring for None presently. In all the world God has glorified Godself, and through all the things of the world God has exalted human beings, placing all earthly things at their disposal. To receive all earthly things placed at one's disposal; what a responsibilty and what a distance from the foundation of consciousness to the perfection of the virtues, what a responsibility. To walk on water and escape the enemy.

It is ringing for None, good Criseldis! There is a dead man lying before the gate, called Ursula to Hildegard. Sick people, beggars, pilgrims, and the dead at our door. Hildegard knelt. He is not dead; bring wine and heat some soup. She struck the man's cheeks. Wake up. She poured wine into him. Wake up, now. She lifted the upper part of his body and propped it against her left leg. Eat, she said, you are not dead and you are not sick, either. She spooned the soup into him. Sit up, now, without support. The man's face took on life; he drank the soup greedily, stuffed bread into his mouth. You are a vagabond, aren't you? The man nodded. Since when? He made a gesture with his hand. Prepare a bath for him, she said to Arnulf, and let him sleep. But I want to talk to him before he goes away. She smelled the odor, saw his unsteady gaze; her hands were sticky. I didn't do this very kindly, she thought, and None is already over. It seems to me as if more and more young people are surrendering themselves to this wandering life, idleness, torpor. Effeminate age.

Write, she said to Hugo:

> Those who so gladly go about as vagabonds have no love for God, nor can God love them. They are lacking in all wisdom, for they do not have sufficient understanding to subject themselves with reverence. They cannot take on any active responsibility unless they submit to love. This wandering is, at the same time, the daughter of disobedience. It is often ac-

companied by sexual immorality. Even if they do not, in fact, fall victim to these things, such vagabonds lust after their society, again and again seek to find them and so submit themselves in service to them. They are either madly enthusiastic or fully lukewarm, or they break loose for any reason at all: in any case, they are like food with too much salt. They cannot produce true joy or genuine sorrow. No word of wisdom touches them, and wisdom herself does not enter into speech with them. They have neither the roots nor the full blossom of a fruitful tree, since neither in the morning does the dew of prophetic enlightenment sink into their roots, nor does wisdom rise into their crowns for edification at midday.

This vice and decay is but foam. It imparts no relish for knowledge and no nourishment in action; it remains faithful to no useful work, and it has neither a watchful mind nor any power to recognize the uplifting of the spirit. Such a vice contains only idleness and torpor, so as to pursue, without plan, its lustful desires and to note only what is changeable, that which crosses its path at every moment. Thus it forgets what belongs to God, and often even neglects the simple needs of the body. Therefore let all those who desire to adhere to God with seriousness and in the joy of life keep themselves far from the vanities of this evil.[9]

Hildegard had spoken more loudly and rapidly than usual, so that Hugo had had difficulty keeping up with her. I don't like the comparison with overly salted food, he said, shouldn't it better be "food without salt?" No, said Hildegard, you can swallow food without salt and be filled by it, but food that is too salty you have to spit out.

She thought of the vagabond, now sated and sleeping, and suddenly she saw Robert: saw him bringing the buckets of mud, laying the mortar on which she set the stones. You must make the layers quite level. She sees his hands, his hair, and sings to put a pair of birds in that hair. Building, she said, is lovely, I could do that all my life. Building and singing. And Robert laughs: you must set the stone absolutely level.

[9] *LVM,* 250–51.

Aren't they often people, I mean the vagabonds, said Odilia softly, who are haunted by world-weariness? That may be, said Hildegard, withdrawing herself from the light of Robert's eyes, that may be so at the beginning, but soon they get luke-warm, even in their sadness. But it is true that those who are world-weary and those who wander about may have a lot in common. World-weariness is also a vice.

> Those who are sorrowful and weary of the world no longer rejoice at the prospect of their heavenly home. This sorrow is like a wind that is useful neither for making things green nor for dryness, since it destroys everything it touches. Hence it has nowhere a proper standpoint. In this way all the powers of life dry up in such persons, since they do not have the breath of the spiritual life within them. Thus this form of sorrow is also divided into different parts, always piling up what is sor-rowful upon themselves and never able to gain true joy in any-thing. They neither speak happily to a friend nor seek to placate an enemy. Instead, they surrender themselves totally to melancholy and creep like a toad into the hole of their heavi-ness, shy of anything they might encounter. But with such an attitude they are more dead than alive, since they no longer look up to their heavenly home, nor do they place any more trust in this world.[10]

The bell rang for Vespers. What should one do to counter world-weariness? asked Odilia softly as they were going out. Trust in this world, whispered Hildegard, sing and pray. You have put gladness in my heart more than when there grain and wine abound. How very good and pleasant it is when kindred live together in unity. It is like the precious oil on the head, running down upon the beard, like the dew of Hermon, which falls on the mountains of Zion. For there the Lord has ordained a blessing, life forever.[11] To ordain life, even here, what a marvelous thing.

[10] Ibid., 258–59.
[11] Psalm 4:7; 133:1-3.

Thorn Thicket

The next day the vagabond had vanished. He took a silver candlestand, two loaves of bread, and two chickens with him, but in spite of this Hildegard went to the daughter monastery as she did every week. On the way to the boat dock she was watching for a ragged figure with a sack on its back. She thought she saw such figures everywhere along the margins of the forest, and she was timid in her greetings to the farmers waving from the fields; she gave a frightened start when Brother Martin stumbled and the horse shied. The moon blushed and the sun was ashamed: she pulled herself together, but she still smelled the odor of the vagabond, saw his shifty eyes.

She was glad to be in the boat, borne along without jolts and jars, tasting the wind and looking at the sky. The ferryman was worried, and she promised him a sheep and a sack of apples; he need only come for them. But she did not arrive punctually for Terce; she sent the waiting sisters away and took care of the sick herself, people who had gathered on the bank; they were more numerous every time. An infected throat, eyes going blind, a swollen abdomen, sores on arms and legs, rotten teeth. I will be a field doctor yet, she thought, and advised, gave orders, made suggestions, stroked, nodded, blessed a newborn child. She came into the monastery for Sext, entered into the ritual, sang a new song with the sisters, repeated a muttered prayer. Her ears and eyes were alert.

After the meal she broke the silence and spoke of Rupertsberg, the apple picking and the vagabond, and she listened to what they had to say, sent the sisters away to rest, and discussed expenditures, income, and repairs with the provost and Margarethe, signed things that needed to be signed, expressed her satisfaction. But when the provost had left, Margarethe began to weep: let me come back to Rupertsberg; I need my sister. Hildegard waited for the real reason. I am not made

221

to be superior over these girls, they are strange to me and I am strange to them. Even Wernhild of Auershausen wants to leave, though she has another reason, she will tell you about it.

This Margarethe of Hohenfels was an energetic woman, enthusiastic about overcoming difficulties. Hildegard laid a hand on her shoulder. Choose someone like you from the house, said Margarethe, you yourself said that one ought not to put oxen and asses in the same stable. It is good for a person not to try to conquer a mountain that she or he cannot move from its place, but to remain in the valley and gradually learn what he or she can do. Yes, yes, said Hildegard reflectively, don't cry any more. The stars cry out, because the moon is vanishing. The valleys make loud lament over the mountains, and the mountains fall into the valleys.[12] I will think it over. Send Wernhild to me.

Put in order all the love in me, she thought.

Wernhild had no problems about status. My legs want to wander and dance, my womb wants to bear children, my thoughts . . . Hildegard interrupted her. Sit down and listen:

> I once saw a figure that looked like a wolf. She squatted on her haunches with her legs crossed, and she said: whatever I can seek, whatever I can wish for, that I will also enjoy. I have no desire at all to restrain myself. Why should one restrain oneself if it profits nothing? Should I forget what I am, when every being insists on its own uniqueness? If I were to live so that I was scarcely able to draw breath, what would my life be worth? I want to grab every kind of play and pleasure that I encounter. If my heart leaps with joy, should I tie it down? If my veins pulse with desire, should I just bleed? And if I am talented in speaking, should I condemn myself to silence? Every impulse of my body will become a true desire! And I intend to live according to the way I am made. Why should I change myself into something different from what I really am? Every creature grows according to its nature, and it acts as is appropriate for it.[13]

[12] See Joel 2:10.
[13] *LVM,* 94.

And that is what you think, too, don't you? Yes, said Wernhild proudly, that is it exactly; that is just what I feel and think.
That is just how I want to live: the way I am made.

> You act [said Hildegard softly] like the young wild beasts who
> as yet know no limits. For everything in God's ordering
> responds to everything else. The stars sparkle with the light
> of the moon, and the moon shines with the fire of the sun.
> Every thing serves something higher, and nothing surpasses
> its limits. But you have regard neither for God nor for God's
> creatures. Instead, you hang in the air like an empty scab-
> bard swaying in the wind. You wear yourself out with your
> attitude, and you will be food for worms.[14]

You need not try to change my mind, said Wernhild, I have
thought it all over carefully for a long time. She lifted her head
and looked Hildegard in the eye. Selflessness delivers us from
the compulsion of self-assertion and from anxiety about our
selves. We are free in our self-emptying, we have loosed our
slavish ties to the world. Hildegard had said this last very softly
and was not certain whether Wernhild had understood. Try
it, and if you want to come back, I will not close my door.
Wernhild went away. Coif and bell, cell and wall. Hildegard
put her face in her hands. Order the love in me!

As she was going past the barns, she met Walburgis. Hair
that heals. You have blackheads around your nose again, said
Hildegard, but Walburgis only laughed. I have two new pots
for the herb kitchen and a pile of freshly cut wooden bowls;
and just look at the hens and ducks, how big they are getting. Hildegard was enchanted with the gleaming poultry. Just
take care that you don't turn the geese into swans, she said.
Do you have anything against our getting some swans for our
pond? "No, the swan loves the earth and all kinds of water
more than flight. Its fat should be used, mixed with mugwort
and oak bark, as an ointment against rashes."[15]

[14] Ibid.
[15] *Naturkunde,* 107.

Hildegard praised the good order and cleanliness, and Walburgis's happy face drove away her sadness. She compared the sheep's wool with that at Rupertsberg, asked Susanna for information about the success of the beekeeping, watched the sisters making candles. To sit here, clean the candles and sing. Candles that do not smoke and smell bad. Why did I never have any luck with beekeeping? You are very industrious and adroit, she said to the sisters in the sewing room. We have invented something new, said Amalie, look how soft these cloths are. They will make diapers for new babies. If you could weave still thinner, said Hildegard, and we cut long strips of the cloth, I would have good stuff for bandages. Would you like to try it? The sisters nodded. One ought not to put oxen and asses in the same stable, thought Hildegard, but it might be better to join the asses.

Another day at Eibingen. Shadows and light. Hildegard stroked the air when she was back in the boat. Late sunshine. Sky dipped in water. Sustain me with flowers, refresh me with apples. Put in order all the love in me. Seal me with his love.[16]

Martin was on the bank with the horse and two mounted soldiers. What is this? There is riff-raff about; we cannot risk it alone. And now shall one of them ride ahead of us and one behind, asked Hildegard, what is this? They could attack you to steal the horse, they could even kidnap the Lady Abbess and ask for ransom. Kidnap me? Hildegard smiled. Tied up and gagged in a hole in the ground, and then Wibert will come and set me free. But then she thought of the vagabonds and her smile faded. They stole the sheep from the ferryman, the one you gave him. They beat up Toeben when he surprised them at his farm. Two maids are supposed to have been raped and tortured. What kind of times are these, when people are afraid for their lives? thought Hildegard. All right then, let's go, she ordered.

What could two soldiers and poor Martin do anyway,

[16] Song of Songs 2:5; see Fox, ed., *Book of Divine Works*, Letter 40, to Wibert and the Monks of Villers, 352.

against a whole band of them? She tried to hum a song, but then she saw the figure with the scythe, and another with a pitchfork. Go on, she said. The horse of the soldier riding ahead shied and reared. The trees swayed in the dusk. A third figure appeared. Even my heart has gone pale, thought Hildegard. Don't be afraid, someone called; we are here to accompany you to the monastery. And now three of them were walking on her right and four on her left, and a crowd joined them. It was a strange-looking procession that approached the monastery. Pitchforks, scythes and sticks on shoulders, dark faces, and rough singing, a song that Hildegard had begun.

She thanked them and went to see about farmer Toeben, who lay sleeping in the sickroom, his skull and hands bandaged. He was lucky, said Clementia; he can go home soon. Alas, what times are these? Berengar has come, said Hugo; you are in danger, that is why we mobilized the farmers. Now they are all alert and ready for a fight; the riff-raff hasn't a chance. You can feel quite secure. How she would have loved to put both her arms around the brother, and around Berengar!

I must sleep, she thought, so that my marrow can grow white again. But she slept badly. Wernhild was hanged on the moon by some threads and was shrieking, her entrails were hanging out of her body, only her skin was still in the air, swinging and crying. A herd of donkeys, dancing, jumping over one another. The moon took on a grey hue. Tugging. Skin tearing. Margarethe with a scythe. She tries to get between them, falls down. They are trampling on her and roaring. They stuff her skin into her mouth, the moon is sailing between her legs.

Hildegard tore herself from sleep, pressed her fists against her stomach, took her bearskin and slipped into the chapel, seated herself on the altar steps. I am an old woman, Rupert, a very old woman, and I am afraid; it is not hard to break through the gate. And what about that business with asses

225

and oxen? The farmers are approaching her, the faces of vagabonds, pitchforks and scythes growing from their foreheads, they are coming nearer and nearer, spitting fire, bending their heads with the pitchforks and scythes, swaying closer and closer toward her on a cloudy world, she flees to the boat but the ferryman changes into a goat. I will ferry you into the abyss, he shouts, and the punt shoots steeply downward, and there are all the vagabonds, all of them, they throw a net over her, pull it tight, drag it through the water, she is choking on the flood. Bawling and roaring, now you are really a feather and no current carries you; they drag the net around and around. Nough-e, nough-e, Gimbert, esaelp, esaelp!

Hildegard woke. Am I then to be burned into lime? Shall I be pregnant with hay and bring forth straw? Alas, the sky is rolling itself up into a ball. I am a broken thornbush. Rolled into a ball and thrown away. What have I done wrong?

How Shall the Islands Rejoice

A short autumn. Burning colors that are extinguished overnight. Trees and bushes beaten empty in a single night, the fields and meadows swept clean. Hildegard stalked through the snow. The graves are covered, the crosses have white trimming. I could probably wear some of that kind of trimming. The collar of the well is white, the summer's blue faded, the crystals dissolve in the hand, the stars flee away. Open the gate and look far away over the white fields. But her wet feet are freezing.

Berengar is singing in the sheepfold, cutting beets. Don't be afraid, it is I, I want to warm my feet. She pulls off her sandals and stockings, and Berengar rubs her feet with straw, calls two sheep and places them so that Hildegard can put her feet between their bodies. Living warmth. Give me a knife, too. The knife is sharp and the rinds are hard, be careful. Listen how it crunches; taste how sweet it is. The sheep get a slice, too. Then they sing together, the blind man and the abbess; they cut beets and sing, the sheep like that, too. It is well with us, isn't it, she says softly; perhaps I will come again tomorrow. She strokes Berengar's face with both hands, pets the noses of the sheep, takes her sandals and stockings and runs back through the snow before her feet can get cold again. Let your happiness shine on all the sisters. A good None. If you offer your food to the hungry and satisfy the needs of the afflicted, then your light shall rise in the darkness and your gloom will be light as the noonday.[17]

Write, said Hildegard, even before she had sat down in the scriptorium:

> The fourth vision gathered itself like a ball of thick smoke into a human form. It had no human limbs, only great, dark, staring eyes. It went neither forward nor backward, moved neither to right nor to left, but remained quite motionless in the darkness. And it spoke: I have produced nothing and brought nothing into existence. Why should I bother about anything or have any cares? I will simply let everything be as it is. I will help people only insofar as they can be useful to me. God, who created everything, should also be there when needed and take care of the universe! If I became involved even the slightest bit in other people's affairs, what good would it do me? I would do no one either good or evil by it. If I were to go around feeling compassion for everyone and everything, I could no longer rest, and what would become of me? What kind of life would I live if I were to try to respond to all the voices of joy or sadness? I know that I myself exist; everyone else should do the same.[18]

[17] Isaiah 58:10.

[18] *LVM*, 33; see Fiona Bowie and Oliver Davies, eds., *Hildegard of Bingen, Mystical Writings,* with new translations by Robert Carver (New York: Crossroad, 1990) 85. Cited hereafter as *Mystical Writings.* Pages 85–89 of this book contain selections from *LVM,* including this passage on the figure called "Hardness of Heart."

Mercy responds to hard-heartedness:

> Oh, you stony being, what are you saying? The plants offer one another the scent of their flowers; one gem beams its brightness on another, and every creature has a primeval drive toward loving embrace. All nature stands in the service of humanity, and in this loving service it rejoices to offer them all its bounty. But you are not worthy even to have the form of a human being. All you are is a cruel and pitiless stare. You are an evil cloud of smoke in the darkness. But I am a soothing herb dwelling in the dew and in the air and in all greening freshness. My heart is overflowing with desire to give aid to each and all. I was already present when the first "Let there be!" sounded, from which came forth the whole creation that now stands at the service of humanity. But all being is closed to you. With loving eyes I observe all the demands of life and feel myself a part of all. I raise up the broken-hearted and lead them to wholeness. I am the balm for every pain, and my words are true, while you remain nothing but a bitter cloud of smoke.[19]

Dark, staring eyes. The voice from the cloud. And then Hugo's heavy breathing. Hildegard was startled; she felt his forehead. You have a fever. Why didn't you say anything? You must lie down, the fever is very high. Then she saw that the jewel in his ring had grown dull, and her heart shuddered.

Clementia and Hildegard took turns. Compresses, poultices, cool hands, medicines, and still other medicines, apple juice, mustard packs, icy air that made the sisters shudder. The nostrils tremble. Helplessness, helplessness. On the fourth day the fever goes down. Clementia nods at Hildegard, but she knows better. His hands are more like their father's hands, his face more like their father's. A park with bending roses. A field where the stars run with you. Don't fight against death. Sleep. You will keep my going out and my coming in. Let me make the clouds my chariot and ride on the wings of the wind. He gives sleep to his beloved.[20] Don't struggle. The

19 *LVM* 34; see *Mystical Writings,* 85–86.
20 Psalm 121:8; 104:3; 127:2.

night air is very light and full of gentleness. The wind is the wings of the cloud chariot. Everything is measured. Sleep.

Three days after Hugo's death the canon died of the same illness. Hildegard was afraid for the sisters, anxious with the strength that still remained to her. Then Hiltrud died.

Hildegard held her dead sister close in both arms. You promised not to leave me; you swore it. Shall I be burned to lime? The sky is rolling itself up like a ball. The mountains are tumbling. How shall we hang our harps on the willows? I will be cut off from the land of the living.[21] You promised. She sways back and forth, wants to sing Hiltrud's favorite song. *O vos angelis,* oh you angels. She chokes. Harps on the willows, only for a little while. She sits silent. Like the wind plucked by the air. Like the frost that screams outside the window. Like the darkness that devours the darkness. The sisters' faces are strange. Then she gives her up, lays her down, folds her hands in one another. Stay seated until the bell rings for Matins. Someone else must keep watch now. Mechthild will take care of everything.

Human beings are like a breath, their days are like a passing shadow. Bow your heavens, touch the mountains so that they smoke. Draw me out of mighty waters. I will sing you a new song, play for you on a ten-stringed harp. Praise befits the upright.[22] Hildegard remains in the chapel after Prime, waiting for them to bring in the coffin. How shall the islands rejoice? My companions are in darkness.[23] Ransom life, how? Hiltrud has a small, grey face, skin and bones. But the hands are tight. It hurts her chin, her forehead, doesn't it? It is injuring her skin. She pushes her head between her shoulders. Jutta is walking on water and the river bears her up. Hiltrud stands there and does not dare to follow her. Come, says Jutta, and Hiltrud places a foot on the water, sets the other in front of it, balances with her arms, puts the first foot in front of

[21] Cf. Psalm 144:5; 137:2; 52:5.
[22] Psalm 144:4-7; 18:16; 33:1-3.
[23] Psalm 88:18.

the second, sinks a little, sinks deeper, strikes out with her arms, calls, but Jutta goes on. Then the floods break apart at last and close over Hiltrud. Draw me out of mighty waters. I will sing you a new song. Hum her favorite song, if you can, says Hildegard to Donata when she takes over the watch after Terce. She goes into the scriptorium.

We must send a letter to St. Disibod. But Odilia writes slowly, very slowly. Her hand is clammy with cold. Hildegard brings a woolen blanket and lays it over her knees, takes off her wristlets and pulls them over Odilia's hands. It takes a long time before the short letter calling for help is finished. Hildegard has to dictate it one word at a time. My tongue is like a board.

As it turns out, the letter is superfluous. Wezelin is at the door. He will come three times a week until a new scribe has been found. He brings greetings from St. Disibod. Uncle Hugo has found a good resting place at Bermersheim. Yes, yes, said Hildegard, we are always wanting to go home, look through the last thing that was written and get ready for the Mass for the Dead. He has a hard mouth, she thinks.

The garden is white, and so is the cemetery. Push the snow aside carefully, she says to the servant who will dig the grave. He does as she says. She feels the earth; it is warm under the snow, and soft. Cover the hole with boards when it is finished, she says. Wild ducks calling. The sky is white. Surely I may be sad. She returns in her own footsteps. She is dizzy. Night follows night. Hiltrud's face. No smoothing out. No light. Only the body swelling up. Hildegard gets her sapphire and lays it in Hiltrud's hands, caresses them. *O vos angeli!* If you have a contract with the stones of the field. Companion of the angels. How I loved your soul. I ask of you, and you grant me my heart's desire. Hildegard sits deeply bowed down. Who turns the rock into a pool of water, the flint into a spring of water.[24] Everything takes time.

[24] Cf. Psalm 21:2; 114:8.

Odilia takes over the watch. Hildegard is alone with Wezelin. Entries in the book of the dead. Write, says Hildegard:

> The sixth figure represents melancholy. Its form is like that
> of a leper and has black hair. For as the lepers live isolated
> from the healthy and pure, so that they may have no contact
> with them, so also the one who is melancholy lives separated
> from all the powers of God and no longer gives off light.
> Nevertheless, the semblance of humanity is preserved. For
> while all other creatures are happy in their obedience to God,
> human beings thrust themselves into the unhappiness of mel-
> ancholy. They exacerbate their situation through the black-
> ness of manifold unnecessary perversions, like tangled hair.
> They do not even blush that they refuse to better themselves
> when they are warned by those who are wiser than they. The
> figure wears no clothes, but merely covers itself with a broad
> cloak of leaves, since it is naked of all the goodness of sanc-
> tity and lives without the joy of salvation; instead, it surrounds
> itself with the inconstancy of every kind of vanity, in order
> through the changeability of its attitudes to grasp at the hap-
> piness that, nevertheless, it cannot have.
>
> With its own hands it tears away the flesh of its breast, since
> it accuses its own conscience, while with its evil deeds it only
> bares the innermost thoughts of its heart. It does not know
> a trusting hope in God, but instead is seized by an evil com-
> pulsion to greater and greater distress, as is clear from its way
> of speaking. And yet, it is restrained by bliss. And people are
> thus taught that they should not continue in a situation of
> melancholy.[25]

Wezelin wrote faster than Gottfried, even faster than Volmar. He did not speak while she was dictating, only wrinkled his forehead now and then. The silence felt good to her.
What are these ways of speaking, asked Wezelin, should they
not be put down here? "What is now my salvation, if not
tears? What life have I, if not pain? And what will be my help,
if not death? What answer will be given me, if not decay?

[25] *LVM,* 113.

There is nothing better for me.''[26] Where does that belong, asked Wezelin. Insert it after ''bares the innermost thoughts of its heart,'' with ''and it says,'' said Hildegard, and felt how the flame struck her in the face. Who answers? Blessedness, said Hildegard. Write:

> From the stormy cloud already described I heard a voice from this figure answering: You are addicted to torment and clearly desire nothing else. God only wishes to be asked, and everyone should seek God's goodness. You distrust your own self because you do not trust in God. You ask nothing of God, and therefore you find nothing.[27]

Stop, cried Wezelin, what kind of monstrous sentence is that: You distrust your own self because you do not trust in God. Yes, said Hildegard, it is a monstrous sentence, but it is correct. Just add:

> But I call aloud to God and receive an answer. I ask of God, and God graciously gives me what I desire. I seek in God, and I find. For in all honourable things I am bliss itself. I strike the harp before God, since I direct all my actions toward God. And so I am seated in God's lap, in my trusting hope that rests in God. But you have no trust in God, and you do not long for God's grace. Therefore only the worst things happen to you.[28]

Could one not formulate that more cautiously, asked Wezelin, are there not other words for grace and bliss, for sitting in the lap, could you not say it with more reserve? No, said Hildegard, that is the way it must be, just write it that way. Weariness is spreading through her. Picking words apart, comparing words, weighing them, arguing. Volmar's big ear, red with enthusiasm. To hang oneself on those ears when the ground falls away under one's feet. I am Volmar, just come

---

[26] *LVM,* 93.
[27] Ibid.
[28] Ibid.

to me when you are anxious about anything. We will imagine the grill away. And when our legs are no longer willing, we will use a chestnut staff. *Aieganz te Liuionz, Ispariz te Inimois!* Days like fleeting shadows. You must capitalize the personal pronouns for God, said Hildegard to Wezelin.

At Compline, Hildegard's face was unchanged. Strained. Dried out. After giving her hand to each sister she covers young Adelgunde, who cannot overcome her homesickness, and sings her to sleep; then she goes back into the chapel. She takes her bearskin, some candles. This night watch is hers. You distrust yourself because you do not trust in God. God turns the rock into a pool of water, the flint into a spring of water. Sing about the angels who protect the peoples, and sleep well, sleep deeply and well. Then Hiltrud's face begins to lighten.

Days
like fleeting shadows,
the harps
hung up
on the willows.

XVIII

Like a Blacksmith

Melting snow. The sun is getting stronger. Piles of wool. Wash it, dry it in the sun, spin great rolls of it. Just look at the summer shirts, says Ortrud; our winter's work. Hildegard feels the material. Isn't it too silky? No, says Ortrud, we only wove it very fine. Not hair shirts, but one could embroider them with thistles or line them with nettles, Hildegard thinks. No offense, but why does everything have to be made more and more fine and elegant? Well, they are really not elegant, but why shouldn't we improve whatever can be improved? Yes, why not? One day you will be making silk stockings, says Hildegard. Ortrud is not laughing now. It is still nothing but raw linen. Hildegard lays a hand on her shoulder: just don't make the linen any finer. Our skin needs friction, that gives it life. We need a living skin.

Living skin. Hildegard's hand circles on the farm woman's abdomen. It is alive. Get rid of it, the woman begs. I have borne thirteen times, I can't do it again, there is no strength left in my back, the children are starving, my husband beats us. Get rid of it. Shall I reach into your belly with my hands and strangle the life out of it, drag it out and throw it in the refuse? No, and again no. You can do it. Hildegard puts her ear against the woman's belly. I can hear it, it is quite contented, and it can already hear us, too. Carry it to term. Then the farm wife stands up and goes away without a word. Alas, fourteen times nine months, fourteen times torn apart, blows and hunger, distress and worry and no more strength remaining. Filth, cold, blows, screams and no more strength. Alas.

Alas, nephew, you have a hard mouth. You are not pious, are you? You on your mountains, says Wezelin, and we in our effeminate age, those are two different things. You can't condemn everyone who is weighed down by the confusion of sin to do penance in a hair shirt. The wages of death leads to greed and quarrelsomeness. Why does he use my words, thinks Hildegard, does he have no vocabulary of his own?

You do not love God. I cannot find God. No one can love what he or she has not found. It is hard, aunt, to be in the world and love a God one cannot find. They have eyes to see, they have ears to hear, thinks Hildegard. They do not know what the world is. And I, a fragile woman, do not know how to teach them. Let us go to work. Write:

> Again I saw other spirits in this crowd, and I heard them crying out as follows: "We do not know who or what God is! We only understand what we see!" These spirits lead human beings to forget God and cause them to be lukewarm in all things. Mindlessness likes to associate with certain beings that know no mobility in good or in evil, but simply lie there in their laziness. It neither fears nor loves God, since it does not taste the fear of God nor correspond to God's love, because it is not at work, like a human being, in the exercise of its reason nor does it pray to God in the breath of its spirit. It comes like a useless puff of wind that dries up the fruits of the earth.
>
> And so it also says to itself: "If there is a God, then God should simply be God; surely God has no need of my efforts. I want nothing else than simply to live." And so mindlessness neglects all good work. A great foolishness has befallen the human being who neither worships nor loves the God who has made all things and whose rule has no end. But wisdom is found in those who, without exception, view in the mirror of the heart the One from whom they have received both body and soul.[1]

Sorceress, says Wezelin, but Hildegard shakes her head. O no, she says softly, not a sorceress, on the contrary. Make straight paths for your feet to follow. Tear yourself away from forgetting God. She stands up, goes to the window, wants to take his head in her two hands. Only wait; I want to bring you into my heart. But Wezelin is already at the door. See you next week, aunt.

[1] *LVM,* 210–11.

Hildegard goes into the garden, filters the water in the well until it is free of dead insects, leaves and foul bubbles. It is time for you to come, Wibert of Gembloux. My time is limited and there is still much to be done. The thrush and the strawberry bed will greet you; in the evening we can sit in the kitchen. This is a great love, we must make use of it. The vineyard is waiting for our steps, the wind for the flying of our habits. Come soon. God is like a blacksmith who blows up the fire with the bellows and turns the tool around and around in it, so that the work may be fully and completely perfected.

The Turning of the Work

They do not know what the world is, and I, untaught, fragile, do not understand how to convey it to them. The flame strikes itself into Hildegard, fires her veins and marrow, blazes up. A sea of flames. A conflagration. Forty days long.

I am not dead, but alive. The sisters carry Hildegard in a chair to the window. She is a light burden. The parts of her body are all dried out, her blood singed like grass. Carry me farther; carry me to the door. The blankets tell her: these are still legs and arms. Mechthild gives her a glass of water. Hildegard recovers her voice, tastes her lips and tongue; she has a proper throat now, and a stomach, too. She breathes; her lungs grow wings. I am alive. The sun puts a nose on her face, she can smell the air and the trees. Now Hildegard gets ears, too, and hears Berengar's singing, the happy cry of the sparrowhawk, and now the wind, too. And then she recovers her eyes and sees the beautiful foliage of the linden and the sky with its blue islands. There is a burning in her eyes, and the sisters turn away. Er-high, er-high, Gimbert, she thinks, I will never again say "nough-e." Carry me to the gate; let me see if the fields have been ploughed. Then the bell rings for Vespers. Let us rejoice and be glad. Out of the believer's heart shall flow rivers of living water. God raises up the poor from the dust, lifts the needy from the ash heap, to make them sit with princes and inherit a seat of honor.[2]

Hildegard ate a little soup, dipped a bit of bread in the wine. She could not yet walk, and her hands lay in her lap, but she was not tired and she did not discourage the sisters' surprise over her; she let them be excited as she waited in her cell. They had not been idle, then; they had not only kept the house in order, but tilled the fields and the garden, carried on the prayers. I give to each the reward that is due to the strength of his or her love. I can be at peace, it seems.

They had practiced the song cycle, the cycle of the virtues. The division of the stage by use of light and shadow was clever. The virtues in white veils, the soul in a white robe, the devil black and wearing a mask. How they sigh over the way of the stranger, the poor human soul, longing for the lost inheritance, lamenting over the burden of the demands of obedience, turning backward and forward between the encouragement of the virtues and the devil's beguilement. "O, I know not what I should do, where I should fly. Alas, I cannot perfect this body in which I am clothed. Come, I will cast it aside." Odilia plays the role excitingly. And Abilgard is the devil; she could be a little more tempting, a little more sneering, but she puts out a hateful scream: "What kind of power is that, that can be no one but God? But I say: I will give everything to the one who follows me and my will.

But you, Humility, and your followers have nothing to give. And all the rest of you? You do not even know what you are!" Young Adelgunde is unbelievable as Humility: "Come to me, you virtues, I will nourish you so that you may seek the lost coin." Donata as Mercy: "I, however, have determined to

[2] Psalm 118:24; John 7:38; 1 Samuel 2:8.

give my hand to all who mourn." Even while falling, fettered, the devil cries, screams and sneers: "But I will hurl you down with my assaults." And finally the rejoicing, and Mechthild saying in a clear voice: "In the beginning all the creatures grew green. In the middle of time flowers bloomed. Then the forces of life declined. This the valiant fighter saw and said: I know this, but the golden number is not yet full. Therefore, glorious Father, look down! I am suffering fatigue in my body, and my little ones are growing weak also. Remember only that the fullness that was created in the beginning should not have faded. At that time you promised that your eye would never turn away until you saw my body full of jewels. For it wearies me that all my members are tumbling down in shame. Father, look, I show you my wounds."[3]

Yes, that is right, thought Hildegard: God's plan and the great, great created world, the human stage with the dreadful struggles between God and the Upstart and the duty to perfect the world through suffering, and to lead the human soul back from confusion. Perhaps I should have written a lot more poetry. The sisters' faces are bright red, their eyes shining feverishly. You did that very well, said Hildegard softly. Thank you. "I, who lie cast down in dreadful timidity, sound a little now and then, like a weak note from the living light."[4] You have caused my note to sound forth in broad spaces, heights and depths. I love you all very much.

[3] Hildegard's morality play, the *Ordo Virtutum,* appears as III. 13. 9 of *Scivias.*

[4] Gronau, 225.

Fair to Me Is My Inheritance

Recovery is slow, the days broken by sleep. A thoughtful look into the kitchens and chambers, at the fire, the doors at evening. Sitting at a sister's bed, opening a clenched hand, stroking a brow, blotting tears. Sleep at night, and during the siesta. Forgetting confused dreams. Sitting at the well, idle, hands in lap, letting her thoughts stray. Waiting for Berengar. Sing something for me.

Stories about magnets, evil, lies, stifled rage. A story about a camel with the power of the lion, the panther and the horse in its hump. About the sturgeon who loves the light of the moon. The vulture keeps watch that no bird should be injured. Stories about the multiplication of the loaves, about Peter who almost drowned. The novices' eyes are bright, their brows wide, mirror of the moon's path.

And then Wibert is at the door. You came riding on a mule, Wibert of Gembloux, did they have no horse for you, calls Hildegard. His arms are rounded gold set with jewels from Tarshish. His eyes are like doves beside springs of water, bathed in milk.[5] And everywhere along the way into the house she says: Wibert of Gembloux has come, Wibert of Gembloux has come and will stay with us, and she takes him with her right away to the chapel for Vespers. *O vos angelis!* A hard "g," a soft "g," a new sound. My chosen portion and my cup, I have a goodly heritage.[6]

The month that is lovely and light and glorious in all the things of the earth, when the mouth finds tasting sweet and delightful, that makes the human heart so happy because all the fruits of the earth are shooting upward to the light and can be seen and grasped by human sight. And the next month, that expands in every direction the fruits that it has brought forth with its mild warmth, and prepares them for ripeness, that shines on the shoulders that undertake every kind of work and so maintain the body as a whole, and lightens the ear, the little wing for understanding words, the portal of the rational soul. And the following month that burns with the full power of the sun, has mighty powers, is full of passion and

[5] Song of Songs 5:12, 14.
[6] Psalm 16:5-6.

241

ripens the fruits of the earth. And the wounded nature of human beings comes to be healed. The living spirit goes forth, becomes a greening body and brings forth its fruit. That is life. That, said Wibert, is what you mean by *viriditas*.

You know it, said Hildegard, it is a creative power. It arises from the elements, lives in the flame, shimmers in the waters, moistens in the stone, abides in the air. It is begotten light that brews all nature to a golden ripeness. It is also in the consciousness, in all knowledge, in the intellect that gives its greening answer. Wibert's gaze encompassed Hildegard's eyes. But do you know, she said, I am afraid, very much afraid, that human beings will make the earth unusable. Yes, I see it coming, she repeated: human beings will make the earth, their own earth, unlivable. See, all things were called into creation for the service of humanity. It felt no disturbance in itself. But when human beings turned to disobedience and opposed themselves to their creator, creation also lost its composure and was dragged along into humanity's unquiet. Write the following, Wibert:

> The elements lament with great cries to their creator. Confused by human sinfulness, they revolve in a strange motion and unnatural circulation, overstepping the proper path that was set for them. Thereby they express the fact that they cannot follow their ways and carry out their natural functions as God has assigned them because they have been made crooked, from top to bottom, by the wicked deeds of humanity. Hence they spread a stink in the pestilential breath of their evil and shameful deeds, like a famine devoid of justice. For human beings do not do these things as they should, since they draw to themselves the smoke of stinking punishments and so participate in the world's stink. For human beings are joined to the elements, and the elements are allied with the human beings. As often as the elements of the world are disgraced by the evil deeds of humanity, God will purify them through human tortures and distress, for God wills that all the world should be pure.[7]

[7] Adelgundis Führkötter, ed., *Hildegard von Bingen: Quellen des Heils* (Salzburg: Otto Müller, 1982) 48; *LVM*, 146–47.

You must underscore the last sentence.

The dictation went better every day, even though Wibert did not agree with the use of such simple Latin. I could really find a more elegant expression, or insert a more impressive stylistic figure, said Wibert. And we should add references to Augustine, Basil, Cassian, Gregory the Great, Origen, and others. But Hildegard refused. I am an uneducated woman; let others do that later. Wibert made such a worried face that Hildegard had to smile, and then she did mention Paul and Mark, Enoch and Elias by name when occasion offered.

After all the other creatures, began Hildegard again after one of the hours of prayer, God created human beings, so that they would find all the things they needed already fully prepared for them. And God enlightened them with the living breath of the Spirit. God secured this wonderful creation in two other ways, so that they might be at the same time both fire and flame: fire in their souls and the flame that flickers forth in their reason. But the flame of reason knew where it should plant the kiss of its choosing. That is the knowledge of good and evil. It does not burn where it does not seek to be active; instead, it flees full of disgust from that which it does not desire to do, unless the artist forces it to burn where he or she wishes to direct it, and the artist sometimes lets it be released at the point where it was desired and where it now burns.

Then, cried Wibert excitedly, the artist has a special role. Yes, said Hildegard, a very difficult one, and sometimes he or she will be broken by it, fall into darkness at least for a time, but it must be done, just as I have said. It is the artist's fate. Then, said Wibert, it is no wonder that it is the artist who is most likely to doubt God, who struggles most sharply with God, and possibly abandons God. That is possible— Hildegard reflected—but he or she is also closer to God than any other; such a one need only wear out his or her skin in order to feel it. Let us take a turn in the garden, begged Wibert, and talk about this more at length. No, said Hildegard, first finish writing: These two powers God places within a fragile vessel in order to accomplish what is adequate and useful to it. And as the fire contains the flame within it, so also the rational human being possesses the ability to act. For the human being gifted with reason first wishes and desires something, and thereafter accomplishes it in some way. But the irrational animal lives as its life is planned for it and can do nothing more because it does not possess the eye of conscious intellect, but rather attends always and only to its own nature.

Flying days, speaking and writing, even in the siesta and into the night. Wibert knows no weariness. Once even Criseldis forgot the time, twelve hours long, but after None Wibert's habit smells of the fields and the sun, he brings a bouquet of grasses with him, a snail's shell, a jay's feather—the jay loves to fly in the storm, it greets favored persons with its cry—brings a blue stone that may have fallen from a star, and Hildegard blushes. Write. Time is fleeting. A call from Gembloux, an order. No, no, not yet. The stars cry out because the moon is fading. Stay, don't go. The stone grows cold in her hand.

Write:

> But as the human being is made up of the elements and the elements are joined into one and none of them can do anything of itself without the other, so also the structures within the human being are unequal, even though they proceed from one and the same breath of life. The dispositions within the human being are fourfold: hard, airy, stormy and fiery. People with hard dispositions are sharp in all things, in all their desires taking no heed of others, but reckoning everything only with regard to themselves. And that pleases them. The moods of those with airy dispositions are continually wavering.
>
> Nevertheless, these people have the fear of God within them, holding their sins in check because they distrust their own deeds. People with a stormy disposition lack wisdom. They mix all their doings with foolishness and are not directed

by the words of wisdom. On the contrary, they are annoyed and dismayed by them. People with a fiery disposition strive toward all that is worldly and alienate themselves from what is spiritual. They flee from peace, and wherever they see it their worldly impulse struggles against it. God knows the arrogance of those who do not look to God obediently. These God will purify with the broom of fear. Through the illness that burdens you God is cleansing your soul, which God desires to lead into its inheritance. You will become a living stone.[8]

The human being and its dispositions, the human being and its stages of life—Hildegard's voice grew livelier—those are not only connected with the life of the senses, the parts of the body, the elements and their qualities, but also with the life of the soul and the life of grace. As one matures, for example, melancholy and reason are subjected to conscience and discretion; then in the next stage planning and provision correspond to the graces of decision and courage, just as in maturity strength and restraint belong together with joy and patience. And desire? asked Wibert.

Desire, said Hildegard softly—desire is already present in childhood, in innocence, before the division begins. A wonderful path, a glorious way it could be, but it is a tightrope walk. And love? Set me as a seal upon your heart, as a seal upon your arm, quoted Hildegard, for love is strong as death. Its flashes are flashes of fire, a raging flame. Many waters cannot quench love, neither can floods drown it.[9] And now come, that is enough for today, I would like to go out into the evening once again, look at the grain and the grapes.

The chestnut staff and Wibert's arm. Thin skin, one foot after another. Just consider the work of the mole. It likes rich earth. "It avoids poor ground, and it throws out what is bad, false and useless. It cannot see because it does not live in the light, but it has great knowledge within and it smells and senses

[8] *Briefwechsel,* 180–81.
[9] Song of Songs 8:6-7.

where it must go.''[10] Miracle upon miracle. Feel how the ears of grain are growing, hear the singing of the ears when you stroke them. Warmth under the thin skin of the feet. Wibert's arm, the chestnut staff. The high sky of summer, evening light, a faraway blackbird. How long our shadows are, soon they will melt into the night. Silence. Nothing about Constantinus Africanus, or Seneca and Pliny and Isidore of Seville. Walking along the foot of the vineyard, not going up or down. My beloved is mine and I am his; he pastures his flock among the lilies. Until the day breathes and the shadows flee. His arms are rounded gold, set with jewels from Tarshish. His body is ivory work, encrusted with sapphires. His legs are alabaster columns, set upon bases of gold. His appearance is like Lebanon, choice as the cedars.[11] We had better go back, says Wibert, the sun has gone down. Hildegard nods. His eyes are like doves beside springs of water, bathed in milk, fitly set. His appearance is really choice as the cedars.[12]

[10] *Naturkunde,* 134.
[11] Song of Songs 5:14-15.
[12] Song of Songs 5:12, 15.

The Bell Is Silent

No, says Hildegard softly, I will not permit them to dig up his corpse again and bury it somewhere like the carcass of a dog. An excommunication is not lifted until the Church authorities confirm it, says Wibert. He confessed, received absolution, took the sacrament from a priest. Is God's assurance of grace not valid? Wibert hears Hildegard's determination and is silent. Is the truth no longer the truth? Night. The moon's face averted. The stars far away. But she knows the paths, the paths to the graves, knows the place, trusts her abbess's staff and the sign. The broom wipes out all traces. No one shall disturb your rest, nobleman. I will not turn aside from the fragile earth, but strive valiantly against it. Let no harm come to your soul. The bell is silent. The Church door is closed. No divine service, no reception of Communion, no song of praise. The sisters mumble the psalms, not hearing one another. The power of the Church.

Bringing in the harvest, milling the grain, crushing the grapes. The bell is silent. No song of praise

Sucking out the birth waters from a newborn child. Giving the deaf their hearing back with her breath. Telling a dying man to get up. Closing Criseldis's eyes. Goodbye, you did well, keeping time punctually for decades; your hands have turned to iron. Don't ring the bells any more in heaven; rest. I will smooth the wrinkles from your forehead, the lines from your lips. *Requiem aeternam et lux perpetua. Ab auditione mala non timebit.* [13]

The anger and sorrow of the sisters. No, I will not allow it. Wearily, Hildegard sets one foot in front of another, she is awkward in using her spoon, the cracks in her voice are constantly growing deeper. Snow encloses Rupertsberg. The bell is silent, the wind.

Her eyeballs are hung to her cheekbones, her lungs nailed to her shoulders. Later, much later, the light.

Write, Wibert. And then I myself will go to Mainz. The horse flies through the wind.

> It is a matter of a dead man whose transferral and burial in our cemetery was done by his priest without opposition. When, a few days after his burial, our superiors ordered us to remove him from our cemetery I was overcome by no little alarm and have, as usual, looked to the true light and, with open eyes, I saw the following in my soul: If, in accordance with your direction, the body of this dead man were to be dug up, its removal would threaten our locality with great

[13] Eternal rest and perpetual light. You will not fear the complaints of the wicked.

danger. It would burst upon us like the black clouds that portend storm and lightning. Therefore we do not presume to remove the body of the deceased, since he had in fact confessed, received anointing and Communion, and was buried without opposition.[14]

Were they listening at all, these gentlemen, did they hear only that they had been subjected to interdict, did they in any way understand the words of her vision? "It is not good for you, because of human words, to neglect the mysteries of my WORD clothed in human nature. Therefore you must ask your prelates to release you from this ban they have laid on you."[15] Only dark faces. How should they comprehend that singing and making music place human beings in harmony with the world above, that one dare not rob God of the honor of the praise that is due? Remain standing, read the letter to the end, into deaf ears.

Fools and madmen, roll up your lives like a weaver. Rolled into a ball and thrown away. You, on the roads of many and various things, you should be forbidden your earrings, they should condemn you to wear hair shirts. Effemeninate age in which God's justice is vanishing. But I will fight against injustice, I will not give up the corpse. I will burn away my wounds with torches. She wept, and the wind shrieked. They are jealous, filled with vengefulness, they want to teach me a lesson, these men, because I am a woman, they want to force me to give in so that they can feel their own power. Alas, the grim eyes.

Wibert, said Hildegard softly, when she had returned to the monastery and sent the disappointed sisters to bed, what is to become of the Church? It is growing rigid with formalities and losing its living breath. It creates discord, outrage, unjust oppression, disharmony. It is driving away the be-

---

[14] *Briefwechsel,* 237; see Fox, ed., *Book of Divine Works,* Letter 41, Hildegard to the Prelates of Mainz, 354.

[15] *Briefwechsel,* 287; see *Book of Divine Works,* Letter 41, 355.

lievers, letting the cross dissolve into drifting smoke that infects and destroys the earth. What will become of it in the decades and centuries to come? And her heart was so heavy that she could weep no more. Wibert was silent, watching her. Tears fell from his eyes. He took her hands and warmed them. Sleep. I am gone like a shadow at evening; I am shaken off like a locust.[16]

[16] Psalm 109:23.

The Mountain of Myrrh

Letters back and forth, back and forth. Finally, the lifting of the interdict. Archbishop Christian of Mainz begs the abbess of Rubertsberg for forgiveness and gentle mercy.

Their feet bear Hildegard to the rope, the bell swings; help me, Mechthild, so that it will sound over the fields and meadows and villages and across the river. Sing, sisters, join your souls and theirs with heaven.

> And again summer.
> The light.
> The wind.
> The islands in the well.
> The fish of the moon and
> the fish of the sun.
> The dill waist-high, the rustling of the umbels,
> the unrolled leaves of the ferns.
> Leave a rose for winter.
>
> And sick people and pilgrims.
> Letters and words.
>
> The contract with the stones renewed.

249

Listen to the birds. They are singing.
Higher and higher.
Earth, fragile, beautiful.

Sisters. Sisters.

It is September 17, 1179. Above the room in which Hildegard of Bingen, at the first glimmer of the Sunday dawn, returned her blissful soul to God, there appear in the sky two very bright bows of various colors. They enclose a long, broad path and extend toward the four corners of the earth: the one stretches from north to south, the other from east to west. At the apex, where the two bows cross, there shines a bright light shaped like the moon. It sheds its light all around and seems to drive the darkness of night out of the house of death. Within this light there appears a shining red cross, small at first, but then growing to enormous size. This cross is surrounded by countless circles of different colors within which form individual, glowing red crosses surrounded by their own circles, but the smaller are the first to be visible. When they have spread across the firmament, they expand farther to the east and seem to descend to earth over the house and to envelop the whole mountain in beams of shining light.

Calendar

1098	Hildegard is born, the tenth child of Hildebert, nobleman of Bermersheim, and Mechthild, his wife, in Bermersheim near Alzey.
1106	Hildegard is entrusted to Jutta of Sponheim, the mistress of the convent attached to the monastery on the mountain of St. Disibod, for spiritual upbringing.
ca. 1112–1115	She receives the veil from Bishop Otto of Bamberg.
1136	Death of Jutta of Sponheim; Hildegard is elected as her successor.
1141–1151	The *Liber Scivias* (*Know the Ways*) is written. The monk Volmar from the monastery of St. Disibod (Hildegard's former teacher) and the nun Richardis of Stade collaborate as secretaries.
1146–1147	Correspondence between Hildegard and Abbot Bernard of Clairvaux.
1147–1148	Pope Eugene confirms Hildegard's visionary gift, having previously ordered it to be tested by a commission sitting at St. Disibod. In Trier, he reads publicly from the *Scivias*.
1150	Foundation of a new monastery at Rupertsberg, near Bingen, to which Hildegard transfers.
1151–1158	Composition of the writings on natural history and healing arts (*Physica* and *Causae et Curae*).
29 Oct. 1152	Richardis of Stade, elected in 1151 as abbess of the convent of Bassum (or Birsim) near Bremen, and having accepted the election against Hildegard's will, dies at the convent of Bassum.

after 1154	Hildegard meets Frederick I in the imperial palace at Ingelheim.
1155	Hildegard, after an illness, rides to St. Disibod, where she demands of the monks that they not withhold from her nuns the lands given to them as their dowries, but that they transfer them to the monastery at Rupertsberg. Abbot Kuno gives her the list of properties. After his death on 24 June, Hildegard negotiates with his successor, Abbot Helenger, over the written commitments and arrangements.
1158–1163	Composition of the *Liber Vitae Meritorum (Book of the Merits of Life)*.
1160	First preaching journey to Mainz, Wertheim, Würzburg, Kitzingen, Eberach, and Bamberg. A second preaching journey in the same year takes her to Trier, Metz, and Krauftal (near Zabern).
1161–1163	Third preaching journey to Boppard, Andernach, Siegburg, Cologne, and Werden on the Ruhr.
1163	Beginning of the composition of the *Liber Divinorum Operum (Book of Divine Works)*. At an imperial court reception in Mainz, Hildegard and Frederick I meet for the second time. On 18 April the emperor extends his imperial protection to the monastery at Rupertsberg.
ca. 1165	Foundation of the monastery at Eibingen above Rüdesheim, which Hildegard visits weekly.
1167–1170	Three years of serious illness; for forty days, Hildegard is entirely confined to her bed.
1170	Fourth preaching journey, to Maulbronn, Hirsau, Kirchheim unter Teck, and Zwiefalten.

1173	Provost Volmar, her secretary, dies.
1173	Completion of the *Liber Divinorum Operum*. After Volmar's death, Abbot Ludwig from Trier and her nephew, Provost Wezelin from Cologne, are her collaborators.
1174	Gottfried, monk of St. Disibod, is sent by Abbot Helenger to be provost at Rupertsberg. He becomes Hildegard's secretary.
1175	Wibert of Gembloux begins a correspondence with Hildegard.
1176	Provost Gottfried, her secretary, dies at the beginning of the year.
1177	Wibert of Gembloux becomes Hildegard's secretary.
1178	Hildegard fights for the right not to have to exhume the body of a nobleman who had been excommunicated but then freed from the Church's ban and buried in the cemetery of the Rupertsberg monastery; the exhumation had been demanded by the bishop of Mainz.
1179	Archbishop Christian takes Hildegard's side. He successfully demands that the interdict placed on the monastery be rescinded.
17 Sept. 1179	Hildegard dies at the monastery of Rupertsberg.

Bibliography

I. German Sources used by the author:

Gronau, Eduard. *Hildegard von Bingen. Prophetische Lehrerin der Kirche an der Schwelle und am Ende der Neuzeit.* Stein am Rhein: Christiana, 1985.

Hildegard of Bingen. *Briefwechsel* [Correspondence]. Translated and annotated by Adelgundis Führkötter. Salzburg: Otto Müller, 1965.

Hildegard of Bingen. *Das Buch von den Steinen* [Stones]. Translated by Peter Riethe. Salzburg: Otto Müller, 1979.

Hildegard of Bingen. *Gotteserfahrung und Weg in die Welt.* Edited by Heinrich Schipperges. Olten and Freiburg: Walter, 3d ed. 1980.

Hildegard of Bingen. *Heilkunde. Das Buch von dem Grund und Wesen und der Heilung der Krankheiten* [Healing Arts]. Translated and annotated by Heinrich Schipperges. Salzburg: Otto Müller, 1957.

Hildegard of Bingen. *Lieder* [Songs] Salzburg: Otto Müller, 1969.

Hildegard of Bingen. *Der Mensch in der Verantwortung. Das Buch der Lebensverdienste (Liber Vitae Meritorum).* Translated and annotated by Heinrich Schipperges. Salzburg: Otto Müller, 1972.

Hildegard of Bingen. *Naturkunde. Das Buch von dem inneren Wesen der verschiedenen Naturen in der Schöpfung* [World of Nature]. Translated and annotated by Peter Riethe. Salzburg: Otto Müller, 1959.

Hildegard of Bingen. *Quellen des Heils.* Edited by Adelgundis Führkötter. Salzburg: Otto Müller, 1982.

Hildegard of Bingen. *Welt und Mensch. Das Buch "De Operatione Dei."* Translated and annotated by Heinrich Schipperges. Salzburg: Otto Müller, 1965.

Hildegard of Bingen. *Wisse die Wege. Scivias.* Translated and edited by Maura Böckeler. Salzburg: Otto Müller, 1954.

II. English works consulted for the translation:

Hildegard of Bingen. *Hildegard of Bingen's Book of Divine Works, with Letters and Songs.* Edited and introduced by Matthew Fox. Santa Fe: Bear & Co., 1987.

Hildegard of Bingen. *Illuminations of Hildegard of Bingen.* Text by Hildegard of Bingen with commentary by Matthew Fox, O.P. Santa Fe, New Mexico: Bear & Company, 1985.

Hildegard of Bingen. *Mystical Writings.* Edited and introduced by Fiona Bowie and Oliver Davies, with new translations by Robert Carver. New York: Crossroad, 1990.

Hildegard of Bingen. *Scivias.* Translated by Mother Columba Hart and Jane Bishop, introduced by Barbara J. Newman, preface by Caroline Walker Bynum. Classics of Western Spirituality. New York and Mahwah: Paulist Press, 1990.

Hildegard of Bingen. *Scivias.* Translated from the critical Latin edition by Bruce Hozeski, with Forewords by Matthew Fox and Adelgundis Führkötter. Santa Fe: Bear & Co., 1986.

Hildegard of Bingen. *Symphonia. A Critical Edition of the Symphonia armonie celestium revelationum [Symphony of the Harmony of Celestial Revelations].* With Introduction, Translations, and Commentary by Barbara Newman. Ithaca and London: Cornell University Press, 1988.

Strehlow, Wighard, and Hertzka, Gottfried. *Hildegard of Bingen's Medicine.* Translated from the German by Karin Anderson Strehlow. Santa Fe: Bear & Co., 1988.